Encounter
A Place Apart

Encounter
A Place Apart

*A Companion for the
Warrior Mystic Monk*

Paul Grout

RESOURCE *Publications* · Eugene, Oregon

ENCOUNTER A PLACE APART
A Companion for the Warrior Mystic Monk

Resource Publications
An Imprint of Wipf and Stock Publishers
199 W. 8th Ave., Suite 3
Eugene, OR 97401

www.wipfandstock.com

PAPERBACK ISBN: 978-1-5326-3337-9
HARDCOVER ISBN: 978-1-5326-3339-3
EBOOK ISBN: 978-1-5326-3338-6

Manufactured in the U.S.A.

This book would not exist without the work and support of Dorothy Gemmel Grout, Jim Stokes-Buckles, and the A Place Apart community.

This guide is put together to assist individuals and groups
to deepen their connection to the lifeforce
that is woven through every created thing,
a presence that is life itself.

Introduction to *A Place Apart*

A Place Apart is a community of people who have found one another through a common longing, through a shared seeking to consciously reconnect our lives to the heartbeat of the lifeforce that holds all creation together. What unites us is neither a physical place nor an institution but a space that is being developed within our hearts and minds.

Now step apart
And become a part
Of all that is
And all that was
And all that was meant to be

www.apartvermont.org
info@apartvermont.org

Contents

Where We Are Coming From

A Place Apart has been birthed from a Christian history. Most of those who relate closely to us see their experience within the church as positive. Many have come to see religion and the institution of the church as inadequate containers for the spiritual awakening that is emerging.

This guide is intended for those who believe that Jesus began something central to the wellbeing of humanity and all creation that has become almost lost within the institution of religion. Many who are embracing this emerging spiritual awakening remain within the church. The church continues to be family. At the same time, one's primary spiritual community is made up of those who are seeking awakening whether they are inside or outside of a religious institution.

> People belonging to any faith tradition could remain in their synagogue, mosque, or church— their religious family—while their primary spiritual community formed within the awakening.

We hope that this guide will be used within churches. Some of this material may be controversial. Given the pace of the current awakening, within five years this will seem tame and after ten years out of date.

Remember that Jesus was accused of blasphemy by the religious establishment of his day. It is likely that you will to some degree be attacked by both the political religious right and the political religious left. Fear is always behind attacks; seek to overcome your own fear. Respond in love, resist pride. All of our knowledge can be inscribed on a grain of sand. What we don't know fills oceans.

To The Church

North American Christianity is on life support. A majority of churches and denominations are being financially propped up by people over sixty. Any significant change within the church threatens its financial base. Religion has become dominated by either the political right or the political left. Expressions of faith within the North American Church resemble the platforms of the Republican or Democratic Party over and against the precepts of the new reign of God introduced by Jesus. The age of the pastor-focused, building-centered church is ending.

> This guide is not about reformation, renewal or revival. Reforming, renewing or reviving what has come to exist is pointless.

At the same time, the world is not a better place without the church. The church will be reborn within a new body. The church has become a chrysalis, the shell that holds the new life that will emerge.

The old shell will need to be broken open and left behind. This will come at a great cost, a death of the old structure so that a new creation can emerge. Spiritual awakening comes at great cost in the short term. Loss is the prelude to everything Jesus is about. Abundance comes in the long term. Remaining where we are comes with little cost in the short term and devastating loss in the long term.

To Youth and Young Adults

Look intently around you. What is working, what is not? Where does lasting hope reside within your future?

This can appear to be a dark, threatening, empty time. This is also an amazing time. Everything must change: politically, religiously, economically, educationally, racially, socially, agriculturally, and environmentally. This is your time. Life and death are set before you, choose wisely, and live joyously.

About This Guide

This study guide is intended for you if . . .

- You are longing to feel more fully alive.
- Your fears, insecurities, and addictive behaviors have been keeping you from breaking out into the freedom and fullness of life that you believe is possible.
- You have come to feel the current directions of political, social, religious, agricultural, and economic systems cannot be sustained.
- You are ready to experiment with practices and disciplines that will help you live creatively and fully.
- You are willing to encounter or re-encounter the life, teaching, and purpose of Jesus.
- You are willing to dialogue with and engage the teachings and practices of Buddhism.
- You are willing to examine the benefits and liabilities of all religions.
- You are willing to not know in order to discover new possibility.
- You can accept and be nurtured by mystery.
- The idea of living as a warrior-mystic-monk resonates with your spirit.
- You can identify with at least one of the following six longings:

    I. I long to be able to slow down; the pace of my life owns my life.

    II. I long to find the true purpose of my life, to find work that has meaning.

    III. I don't want to feel afraid anymore, of what might happen, of what people think of me, of life.

IV. I long to find a place where I truly belong, where I am loved and where I can love.

V. I don't want to just live on the surface of life. I want to go deeper. I want to live deeper. I want to be more real.

VI. I know there is more to life. I want to know how to begin seeking. I long to find others who will seek with me.

How to Use This Guide

This is NOT a study guide in any traditional sense. The purpose of this guide is NOT to bring about stimulating discussion related to the themes of the various lessons.

Discussions too often degenerate into subtle debating sessions in which individual opinions are expressed for the purpose of coming up with the "right" answer. The "right" answers tend to be awarded by default to those with the most persuasive power. "Right" answers are too often the domain of those seeking power, or of those who seek easy comfort.

Entry into this material demands a spirit of seeking, an attitude of not knowing.

Meditation Exercises

At the conclusion of each lesson a meditation exercise will be suggested to nurture an engagement with the material encountered within each lesson in a spirit of mindfulness.

Although many benefits can be ascribed to meditation, we are primarily looking for one. Our purpose is to begin to take some control over the constant chatter of judgments, opinions, preconceptions, and thoughts that invade our minds. Relinquishment of all that is no longer serving us is at the heart of this guide. Relinquishment of thoughts that take control of our minds, robbing us of clarity and peace, is central to creating a childlike state of mindful openness to the changes that must occur if we are to experience awakening.

Don't Just Seek, Find

Don't Just Try, Do

Much of the material in these lessons is about seeking new understandings and trying new paths. The problem with an attitude of seeking is that seeking in itself can become the goal. Through seeking we can discover new truths and feel satisfied simply by the discovery without stopping to fully live within those truths. We become seekers, we even become finders but somehow not livers.

We can try new paths without fully embracing any path. We live within a culture that is always looking for the next new thing, trying the new thing without ever fully doing the new thing. We become tryers not doers.

These meditation exercises attempt to stop us, stop our conscious seeking, stop our conscious trying. In meditation we learn to shut off the mind's chatter, analyzing, judging, seeking, trying.

> In meditation we operate within arrival, we live within now, we give ourselves to the moment we are in. We are setting the stage for a lifetime of being within each moment.

A Note on Icons

On the facing page of each encounter is an icon designed for *A Place Apart*'s focus on connecting to the presence of the lifeforce within the teaching, life, and mission of Jesus and seen throughout every aspect of creation. We encourage the reader to regard icons as windows to be looked through toward a deeper level of understanding. The icon does not attempt to tell a story but to arouse a sense of our place within the interconnected story of the lifeforce visible through all of creation.

Getting Started

Belief Systems

Belief systems dominate the way we perceive the world. Where we live in the world, our race, our gender, our family, our culture, our sexual orientation, our government, our political affiliation, our religion, our social and economic standing largely determine what we believe.

There can be no spiritual awakening without daring to question the systems we give allegiance to.

It is extremely difficult to move beyond the dominating influence of these systems of belief. To even begin to question these systems demands some sense that they are no longer working for us, are perhaps working against our wellbeing and the wellbeing of the world we live in.

A feeling of loss often emerges as we begin to question our long held beliefs. It is the function of these systems to make us feel safe, they offer a sense of security and belonging. Belief systems offer a sense of control; of rightness. Often clung to for a lifetime, we come to believe our system is right while other systems are wrong. Almost all belief systems are dependent upon naming other systems as wrong or evil.

There is a sense in which all belief systems work to some extent and have been necessary within human development. Over time systems develop mythologies that are portrayed as history to perpetuate the institutions and the power of those that run them. We live in a time when these institutions and the systems that prop them up threaten to imprison our spirits and take our world to the edge of destruction.

This guide begins by seeking to take us to a place apart,
a place of questioning, to a place of daring to not know.

The core question within the prelude to a new beginning is asking how systems we give allegiance to may work against a spiritual awakening. The first lessons within this guide will seek to help us take a fearless look at the belief systems that order our daily lives.

Awaken

A Place Apart has produced these encounters to give direction to individuals and small groups seeking to more deeply embrace a spiritual awakening that is emerging across religious, political, cultural, racial, gender, sexual, economic and social divides.

Spiritual awakening and our survival as a species have become intractably linked. The future of human life on Earth, at least the quality of human life, will depend on our spiritual advancement catching up to our technological advancement.

A great awakening is being driven by a great human emptiness. For the most part, we know that something is dangerously wrong in the world. Our emptiness is foundationally a spiritual emptiness. Humanity's obsession with technological and material advancement—apart from spiritual advancement cannot be sustained. Emptiness and fear are byproducts of this advancement, emptiness and fear that neither a Bronze Age tribal religion nor a self-centered secular humanism is able to abate.

The Seeking Community

We come together to form a community of seekers. We seek together a depth of living that we have not been able to sustain on our own.

We come together as ones whose different forms of addiction control and devalue our lives. Our addictions can be to drugs and alcohol, to religious, political and philosophical belief systems, to material things, to fossil fuel, to food, to fear, to self, to others. We confess that the gods of our own invention and the god of self cannot save us. We seek together a power beyond ourselves.

We also come together in a spirit of hope and thankfulness. We celebrate the blessing of life, the gifts that each of us has been given and the gifts of one another that will be encountered through this gathering together. We celebrate that we are able to envision something more for our lives.

A Few Guidelines

We welcome all faith traditions along with those with no religious affiliation.

No religion will be promoted. (Refer to "Where We Are Coming From," page 1)

If you believe that a particular philosophical, religious or political belief system is the only right and true way of believing, these encounters are not for you. This does not mean that no clear path will be embraced; it just isn't going to be a religious, political, or belief system path. The emphasis here won't be on what we believe, but upon how we will decide to live.

If you personally and the culture you live within is not seen by you as in desperate need of spiritual awakening and transformation, this guide is not for you.

Where are we going?

We have many clues related to our becoming fully alive; at the same time it is often clearer what must be walked away from than what must be embraced. Refer to the table of contents to find the themes that will be encountered.

Belief Systems and Jesus

The life and ministry of Jesus questioned the belief systems (religious and political) of his day. He saw how the assumptions of those belief systems degraded human life.

Jesus' radical involvement with outsiders, with women, with the poor, with the despised, with those deemed by the system to be unacceptable was in itself a confrontation of the agenda of the religious and political systems of his day and those it empowered.

It is understandable that the foundational systems of his day, religious and political, conspired to put Jesus to death.

Following the death of Jesus a new community was formed. Love was its foundational principle, which included the love of enemies. These early followers of Jesus adopted a communal lifestyle and a shared economy. They prayed together daily and remained part of the religious establishment as long as they could. Women held an equal standing in the new community. Social and economic standing was to hold no advantage.

Within a relatively short period of time this new movement became institutionalized. The old belief systems were interchanged with new ones. Beliefs became institutionalized. The most powerful and influential determined what was good and what was bad, who was in and who was out. Women lost their equal place. Within three hundred years, the new religion that was formed became the exclusive religion of the empire.

Now, 2000 years later, the transformation of humanity that Jesus began in order to save humanity from its mad march to destruction must be revived for the sake of all life on Earth.

Now It Begins
And We Are Here Together

The fading light
   The deterioration of our senses
      atrophied spirits
      mummified souls
      the blindness
      the deafness
    does not occur quickly

We do not wake up one morning
suddenly unmindful
of all that the lifeforce lays before us
minute by minute
hour by hour
day by day

    The numbing occurs over years
    our senses shut down over decades
    minute by minute
    hour by hour
    day by day
       our aliveness diminishes

We were born human beings
we die lawyers, bankers, teachers
    doctors, secretaries, ministers, clerks
    with blue collars or white collars
    always collars
We were born human beings
We die republicans or democrats

Catholics or Protestants
Muslims, Christians, Jews, Buddhists
liberals
conservatives,
progressives
intellectuals
artists
secular
fundamental
evangelical
spiritual
political
Whatever we are
we are different from "the others"
we have it right
they have it wrong
We buy it
we sell it

and it is all the same thing

we are right
they are wrong

We cover over our emptiness
with our rightness
and their wrongness
with busyness
with consuming
with sex
with food

We drug ourselves
with opinions
philosophies

We shoot up

with religion
the system
always the system
the lies
the lie

And always the fear
am I doing it right?
do I look alright?

Why can't I shut off my mind?

Am I pretty enough?
strong enough?
young enough?
old enough?
athletic enough?
smart enough?
Am I good enough?

Why can't I shut off my mind?

AND IT ALL ENDS NOW

We are just plain sick of it
sick of the lie
sick of the game
sick of the systems
sick of ourselves
sick of the maintenance
sick of being afraid

The yearning
the longing
the aching
to be alive
begins

to overpower
fear
I will begin here
I will no longer be afraid
of being afraid
Now the healing begins
now the curtain is torn
now the veil is lifted

He is opening our eyes
spit and mud
water and blood
He was before creation

She hovered over primeval waters

And always I AM

The ancient teaching begins anew
the darkness
the light
the shadow

Again the mystery

and we come not knowing
vulnerable
poor
seeking

dancing

Into the light
the darkness
the shadow
the mystery

Into life

Creator
creation

plant
animal

solar system
galaxy
universe
universes

he
she

ALIVE

NOW IT BEGINS
AND WE ARE HERE TOGETHER

Applying the Encounter to Our Lives

- Reread the introduction material at the beginning of the guide. Reflect on what is being said. Reflect on what is being asked of you.

- Read the 12 Steps of Alcoholics Anonymous. Are these steps at least symbolically applicable to the present human condition, to your present condition?

- Make a list of the systems of belief you encounter in your everyday life.

- How have the culture and family you grew up in, the things you have experienced and the genes you were born with been both a gift and a liability in your life?

- What is your deepest fear?

- What is your deepest hope?

- How do current events in local, national and world news reflect the spiritual condition of the world.

- Are there books you have read or films that you have seen recently that reflect the spiritual condition, or perhaps the spiritual hunger within the world?

Meditation Exercise

Set a timer for one minute. Sit on a chair in an erect position with knees bent so that the bottoms of both feet are flat on the floor. It can be helpful to your posture to roll a bath towel and place it behind the small of your back to enhance the natural arch of your spine.

As you begin the timer meditate on the word *AWAKEN*. Do not think about how to awaken, simply give yourself to the word awaken. Through the next sixty seconds surrender this time to an awakened state with no evaluation of what this means and accepting that you don't know.

This one minute exercise will reveal what little control we have over our mind's intrusion within every moment. To be able to control fruitless, mindless thinking for just one minute can in itself be the beginning of awakening.

Repeat this exercise daily until the next encounter.

Is God Real?

There have been times in human history when the designation for God was too holy to be spoken. Instead an audible breath would be exhaled in deep respect, mystery, and awe.

It is understandable that humans came to picture God in a human form. This form made God more explainable and perhaps more approachable. The problem is that it also made God more definable, and whoever possessed the power at any given time in history got to do the defining. This on some level explains how God over time became an all-powerful man.

Spiritual awakening demands a fearless look at the gods we have created and how these creations hinder our spiritual development.

NO

The question, "Is God Real?" if answered in a literal way is no, God is not real. God is a Bronze Age male deity who visits Earth periodically to grant favors to those who believe in Him in the right way or to dole out punishment on those who don't believe in Him in the right way.

God is sixtyish, dressed in a white flowing robe with long white hair and a white beard. God lives in heaven and lets people into this domain after they die if they believe right, and sends those who don't believe right to hell.

This is a god who humans created in their own image, a god who supports unspeakable acts of cruelty, the death of whole tribes and races of people; men, women and children who are deemed to be on the evil side of history in particular times and places. In Encounter 13 we will examine the problem and depths of evil within the human experience and the role of spiritual awakening in understanding the sources and effects of evil.

Throughout history God supports people who hold power. Kings sponsor translations of scripture. Masses of people are kept in check because God favors rulers, their wars, palaces, treasures, decisions and lifestyles. To go against rulers is usually synonymous with going against God.

God is jealous, moody, loving or benevolent dependent on his mood. God is put in a bad mood if people dishonor him by doing bad things, or not believing in him, or not worshipping him. God is put in a good mood if people honor him by doing good things, by believing in him and him alone and by only worshipping him alone.

God's greatest archenemy is Satan. God and Satan are continually battling to win the hearts, minds and souls of people.

Millions upon millions of people are leaving this God, which is quite understandable. *But where are they going to go?* This God, and variations of him, is the only God most people, believers and nonbelievers know.

Throughout history understandings of God have experienced change or moderated but this human male image lies deeply ingrained in our consciousness. We can attempt to reform him, reinvent him, de-sex him, make him a mother and a father, but through it all God seems to stubbornly remain God.

So people leave God and the religion that promotes him. But what fills the void? Is the world a better place without God? Is the world a better place without religion? Perhaps it is, but what fills the void of churches, synagogues and mosques?

The Great Question

If God is a human invention there remains a great question. Why did humans invent him? There are many possible answers. Humans needed something to explain the mystery, needed something beyond them to feel safe in a world that could be very dangerous. They needed something to deal with the loss and fear experienced through death.

Tribes of people wanted to feel superior to other tribes; "Our God is stronger than your God." Male Gods were often the choice of male-dominated city-centered nationalistic societies while female gods were often the rage of hunter-gatherer, livestock-raising fertility-focused groups of people.

Darker reasons exist for sponsoring God. Unspeakable acts of violence need to be excused; "God told me to do it."

With all the possible reasons that exist for the invention of God, there remains one overarching explainable reason. Human beings have throughout their history perceived an unexplainable force existing that continually appears to be operating just beyond their ability to explain. This is something that we cannot quite touch, or see, or smell, or hear or taste but seems still to exist just beyond our human senses.

What can make this more puzzling to us as humans who generally feel superior to all other life on Earth, is that birds and animals, fish and insects, plants and all other life on Earth seem to be in tune with this force and are able to access it in ways that we cannot begin to comprehend.

There is a motion and direction and life within all created things that their brains and their biological physical make up do not explain. Every created thing around us seems in tune with and content within their surroundings except us. Why is this?

Thousands of years ago humans tried to explain this dilemma, this something that had been lost from their very beginning. In the book of Genesis, within the first three chapters of this first book of the Bible a profound human interpretation of what had been lost is recorded. We will deal with these three chapters in Encounter 3 of this guide.

Yes

There are dimensions to the universe, to the world we encounter daily that we cannot see but we know are there. A train whistle blows miles away from us and flows to our ears on waves of sound that we cannot see. Unseen waves of light hold visual and audio messages that can only be accessed through complex receivers turned to particular frequencies.

We are constantly in the presence of billions of messages carried on waves we cannot see or hear and rarely consider. Only the instruments that receive, decode, transmit and project these waves reveal their presence. The waves have existed throughout human history but only in recent history have we discovered them.

Our advanced technology is still capable of seeing only a tiny portion of the universe. Science has advanced to the point that humans are now capable of beginning to understand how little we know, how much of what goes on within our bodies, throughout the Earth, our solar system, galaxy and universe is beyond our present comprehension.

There is an unseen ever present web of connection flowing throughout the Earth, within our bodies, within every created thing, connecting us to every created thing.

Unseen energy, filaments, streams, strings of light are alive within every cell of our bodies, alive within every cell of plants, animals, insects, trees, soil, water, the Earth, solar system, galaxy, universe, universes.

This energy never dies but continually takes on new form. The energy is not seen; only its manifestations within every created thing is seen. This energy, these unseen filaments, vibrations, strings of an unknown light, connect to a great web of consciousness woven through and beyond the cosmos.

It would take millions of years traveling at the speed of light to reach our closest neighboring galaxies, but we are within every moment connected to the most distant realms of the universe by the invisible web that flows through the cosmos and beyond, holding all that is in its benevolent embrace.

We cannot at this time consciously detect this presence. The course that humanity has taken has separated us from this embrace. We are imprisoned within rooms of our own making whose doors have always been open.

Buddha

Two thousand five hundred years ago, five hundred years before Jesus, the Buddha sought to find a way of emptying himself of his mind's domination over his life and the constant suffering this caused him. He determined that human beings were imprisoned by thoughts they had lost the ability to have any control over.

The Buddha realized that his mind's constant barrage of judgments, longings, fears and desires forced a focus on the future and past that robbed him of any real peace within the present.

The Buddha set out upon a long journey that would clear his mind of the thoughts that had held him captive and upon a path of mindfulness that led to his enlightenment.

He taught others of this path to enlightenment that was created by living mindfully within each moment of ones life as each moment was encountered.

It will be helpful for those seeking spiritual awakening to participate in a dialogue with Buddhism.

Jesus

Five hundred years after Buddha, Jesus can be seen as teaching a similar emptying. For Jesus the emptying focused on the self, and those things that we obsess on, desire and constantly seek for ourselves to fill a deep emptiness. This constant desire for more can never be filled.

It is possible that Jesus, prior to the beginning of his public ministry had experienced the teachings of Buddhism.

For Jesus, the self-emptying provided a space for filling ones emptiness with a presence that would allow for a new self to emerge. Through this emptying of the domination of the old self and the filling of Spirit, the new self, the originally ordained self would emerge. The fruit of this Spirit was Love, Peace, Joy, Kindness, Patience, Goodness, Self-Control, Faithfulness, Gentleness; the fruit would both bless the self and the world one walked within.

Jesus constantly attended to his own mindfulness and his connection to Spirit. He continually sought out the wilderness and quiet places for extended periods of refocus.

Jesus' connection to a power beyond himself empowered his life and the lives of those who followed him. Jesus was the firstborn of a new species of humanity. More of this will be reflected on in *Encounter 5: Jesus, the Firstborn of a New Humanity.*

Applying the Encounter to Our Lives

- How might one's belief in God block one from a spiritual awakening?
- How might one's not believing in God block one from a spiritual awakening?
- How is an understanding of Buddhism central to a spiritual awakening?
- How is an understanding of the life and teachings of Jesus central to a spiritual awakening?
- Can you identify thoughts that continually come into your mind that work against your happiness and well-being?

    How is your mind your friend?

    How is your mind your enemy?

- Do you believe in a power beyond yourself? If so how might you describe that power to someone else?
- How is technology a gift in your life?
- How is technology a curse in your life?
- How might you begin taking steps on a path that could bless your life, the lives of those you love and the lives of those in need?

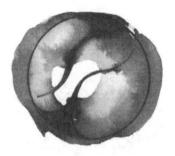

Meditation Exercise

Set a timer for two minutes. Sit in a comfortable posture conscious position. Begin the timer and again meditate on the word *AWAKEN*. Through
the next two minutes give yourself permission to stop evaluating, judging,
planning ahead or looking back. Let the word awaken and that word alone
fill your spirit without filling your mind.

Repeat this exercise daily until the next encounter.

The Beginning

Genesis 1-3

The first three chapters of the Old Testament set the stage for the entire Bible and to some degree set the stage for these encounters. There emerges in these few chapters a profound truth about the human condition. A relationship to creator, to creation, to one another has been lost; and it cannot be regained.

Although parts of this creation story no doubt reference ancient stories, this creation account was set down by an established nation with an established religion. This was likely being composed at a time in Israel's history when everything was falling apart. This is precisely why it is so important to us now.

First we must get over thinking that these chapters have anything to do with a scientific or historical explanation of creation. Genesis one through three make no attempt to even appear historically or scientifically true. In chapter four Adam and Eve have two children, Cain and Abel. After Cain kills Abel he goes off, gets married and founds a city. Even little children ask where all the people came from if Adam and Eve are the first human beings.

This story and almost all other stories within the Bible reveal deep truths and at the same time reveal the agenda of those who set them down. Those who defend these stories as absolutely historically and scientifically true are in positions of power or denial that they are invested in clinging to.

Right from the start of the Old Testament, it is almost impossible not to see God as a dominant, superhuman male. He forms Adam like a sculptor would from clay. This may for some be a beautiful metaphor of how we came into being but if read historically/scientifically a case can easily be made for God being a superhuman male. This tragic approach to understanding and defending the Bible limits if not destroys our potential for spiritual awakening.

God did not create the world in six days and on the seventh day rested. This story was the creation of a religious establishment holding up the importance of the Sabbath.

Read this story again. This is our story. Once we were naked and not ashamed, all our needs were cared for, everything laid before us was good, and we messed up and lost it all and we can't seem to find our way back.

The Garden

Our Original Union

Adam and Eve represent all humanity. They were created within a garden where all their earthly needs were supplied. Everything was taken care of. They were naked and not ashamed. Their creator had taken care of everything for their wellbeing and was always close at hand.

The Fall

Our Great Separation

One condition was set by the creator of humanity. In the Garden of Eden, they could eat the fruit of any tree; "But from the tree of the knowledge of good and evil you may not eat, for the day that you eat from it you shall surely die."

Eve is tempted by the serpent, by the desire within her being, within the being of all humanity, to be in control, to have what we want no matter what the cost. She is told, "You won't die if you eat the fruit, in fact you'll be like God if you eat it."

With all that humanity is given, we want more; we want the control over life, over all creation, that the fruit of the tree of the knowledge of good and evil promises us.

Knowledge without wisdom degenerates into curse. The immediate power that the fruit provides is nearly impossible to resist, no matter what its consequences.

Now we will determine who and what is good, who and what is evil; who and what is right, who and what is wrong. And always we are good and right; our opinions, our tribe, our nation, our religion is good and right and those not like us are evil and wrong.

The knowledge of good and evil demands our finding and naming the good, demands our finding and naming the evil.

And violence is always the consequence, for the good must be promoted and established at all cost, and the evil must be railed against and destroyed at all cost.

Eve takes the fruit from the tree and she and Adam consume it together. That which was forbidden had become the focus of their desire and the source of their separation from God, one another, and all creation—their death.

For the first time they experience shame.

Jesus

From Death to Life

After eating the fruit from the tree of the knowledge of good and evil everything changes for Adam and Eve. They have lost life as life had been created to be. They are banished from the garden. The garden has been sealed off and there can be no return. But they do not immediately die; or do they?

The death that Adam and Eve have been warned of is not at first physical. The essence of what is lost for humanity in our mindless rebellion is the fullness of life that is possible for us.

Because of the way we have been conditioned to think about God, when we think of separation from "him", we almost cannot help but think of a hurtful break from a father figure. In the case of the first three chapters of Genesis it is difficult not to imagine that God is mad at Adam and Eve, mad at us because we broke the rule; we were naughty, sinful and disobedient and God is very disappointed in us.

But suppose God isn't just a superhuman being. Suppose what we have imagined, named and determined God to be isn't about God so much as about us. Is it possible for us to imagine a lifeforce that generates, sustains, inhabits, perpetuates, nurtures and envelops every created thing? Separation from this lifeforce means separation from life as it was created to be. We are separated not because the lifeforce broke off with us, we broke off on our own. We were not banished in punishment, we simply no longer belonged, we went our own way, from connection to control, we ate the fruit and became our own god. Genesis 1-3 makes that into a parable.

Please try to hear this. We are afraid of death because we are no longer connected to life, we are no longer connected to the unifying web, the throbbing heartbeat of the Spirit, the healing presence of the lifeforce. We by our own choices are banished from Eden.

Once, long ago, we lived within the rhythm of the heartbeat of life. Our loneliness is driven by the longing of our memory. There existed, even in recent times, enclaves of cultures who lived within this rhythm of connection. These cultures have been destroyed through the centuries by the global conglomerate of religion promoting a God in a far off heaven. That God and its functionaries profit from our fearing death.

All creation lives within the rhythm of the heartbeat of the lifeforce except for us. Once we were naked in the garden and not ashamed. Now we have become overwhelmed by our self-absorption and we stand alone and ashamed in our nakedness. The beauty of creation is being destroyed by the global conglomerates of religion in contemporary culture worship; whether Christianity, Islam, Judaism, secular humanism, corporations or empire.

Jesus comes to Earth to resurrect us from death to life. He says of himself; "I am the resurrection and the life." He reunites us to the lifeforce that holds all creation together.

The purpose of Jesus is *NOT* to get us *INTO* heaven after we die. He says of his coming; "I have come so that you may have life, and have it abundantly"

Life is available to us now.

Awaken
Life is meant to be full
Dare to live it.

Our souls have been damaged
By a culture that demands our attention
In every waking moment.

Now step apart
To become a part
Of all that was
And all that is
And all that is meant to be.

Applying the Encounter to Our Lives

- Read the first three chapters of Genesis as if this in some way was your personal family history told in an imaginative way.

- After eating the fruit, Adam and Eve are confronted by God. God knows something is up because they are trying to cover up their nakedness. Eve blames the serpent who tempted her. Adam seems to ascribe 50% of the blame on Eve and 50% on God (who created Eve in the first place). How is this blaming a result of eating the fruit?

- Try to put into your own words what the knowledge of good and evil actually is.

- How is it possible that this knowledge can do such great damage to our lives?

- If the garden is sealed off and there is no hope for return, where is hope to be found?

- What is it that Jesus is offering? This will be the main question throughout these encounters.

Meditation Exercise

Take control of your mind. The beginning of freedom is the ability to control our minds. The tempter is our mind, and we are continually being played.

Meditate for three minutes in hope. Do not think about the meaning of hope, or about how to find hope. Do not discuss hope in your mind. Do not think about hope. Attempt to let no words or thoughts form in your mind.

Set a timer for three minutes and sit in hope. Let hope wash over your being like a mist, but do not even seek to picture a mist.

Repeat this exercise daily until the next encounter.

The Bible

The Bible is a compilation of books divided into two Testaments; the Old Testament containing the sacred texts of Judaism and the New Testament containing the sacred texts of Christianity.

Although Christianity includes the Old Testament within its scripture, the New Testament with its focus on the life, teachings, death and resurrection of Jesus is seen as a special revelation that both blends with the Old Testament and supersedes it. For Christians the Old Testament is read in the light of the revelation of the New.

The Bible contains some of the most ancient writings that have survived through human history. The Bible has been a great gift to humanity.

The Bad News

Tragically there is a dark side, the Bible has also been used throughout history to justify despicable acts that have greatly damaged humanity. Wars have been fought, genocides have been perpetrated, great violence has been done, races of people have been subjected to slavery, women have at times been regarded as little more than slaves, all justified by interpretations of the Bible.

The Bible has been used by unscrupulous people throughout history to gain and hold power. The Bible has been used by good people, who seek the betterment of society, to impose their religious agenda for what they see as the good of humanity. At this time in history perhaps the greatest tragedy related to the Bible is the increasing number of people who have turned away from it or who will never read the Bible because of the way the Bible has been so abusively misused by so many.

Vast numbers of people have come to believe that the Bible is not true because of the arrogant claims of certain religious groups. Perhaps the most dangerous claim is that the Bible is inerrant, that every word is true. This claim magnifies our human fallenness, and the self-deception we are capable of as it was depicted in Genesis through our eating of the fruit from the tree of the knowledge of good and evil (refer to Encounter #3). Believing that we completely understand the words of God makes us gods.

Stories within the Bible reveal deep truths and at the same time reveal the agenda of those who have set them down. Those who defend stories as absolutely historically and scientifically true are in positions of power or denial that they are invested in clinging to. The Bible, if read with almost any political, religious or social agenda, can be used to prove and justify that agenda.

Science and the Bible

Science and religion have had a troubled relationship. Throughout history, discoveries in science that cast doubt on the scientific and historical accuracy of scripture could put the discoverers in great jeopardy.

Early astronomers were often imprisoned, tortured and threatened with death if they did not recant their heretical discoveries. The astronomer priest Giordano Bruno was executed because he adamantly clung to his belief that the sun did not make a daily rotation around the Earth. The idea that the Earth was not at the center of the universe threatened the "truth" of scripture. The Old Testament describes an incident in which God stops the sun's movement in the sky to benefit his people in battle. The sun's rising and setting is frequently spoken of in scripture. Over the past several hundred years religion has come to an uneasy acceptance of the sun's stationary place in our solar system. The size and age of the universe is another matter entirely.

Millions of Christians still cling to the literal scientific and historical truth of the creation story in Genesis; believing that the Earth was created six thousand years ago. This is so adamantly defended in the face of over-whelming evidence to the contrary because of the perceived threat to the Bible's truth.

Perhaps the most damaging modern battle between the defenders of religion and the defenders of science emerged with the publication of Darwin's theories of evolution. The battle over evolution and Biblical truth continues to this day. Christians who hold political power in many areas of the country can still dictate what will appear in school textbooks according to their religious beliefs. The message from religion seems to have been that the Bible's truth and scientific truth are incompatible.

If the Bible's truth is dependent on scientific and historical accuracy then the Bible is not true. If many religious laws recorded in scripture are not relevant to today's understandings does this mean that the Bible is irrelevant in today's world?

The bad news is that the Bible is not what so many have claimed it to be. It is often in the interest of religious institutions and those who hold power within them to defend their own literal interpretations. Defending the inerrancy of scripture is a veiled justification of one persons or one group's interpretation. When the Bible is read and defended in this way the potential for spiritual awakening is all but obliterated.

The Good News

The good news is that the truth found within the Bible has never been dependent on its historical or scientific accuracy. There is no story within the Bible that is dependent upon this kind of accuracy. Truth is revealed within the Bible's universal understanding of the human condition.

Every law, every spiritual practice, every poem, every prophecy, every historical event, feast day and festival, every proverb and parable can reveal a timeless spiritual truth.

The truth of the Bible is revealed to those who come to it genuinely wanting to live in a way that will bring blessing and peace to their individual, family and community lives.

The Bible is a healing balm for those who come to it longing to be well.

The good news is centered upon a person, not a book. For the followers of Jesus the Bible is not at the center of their faith, Jesus is at the center. The Bible is to be read in light of the life, teachings, death and resurrection; the way, the truth, and the life of Jesus.

Placing faith in the Bible gives too much power to those who are interpreting. We so easily interpret with our own particular interests in mind. The Bible contains sacred truths, but the book's sacredness is dependent upon the sacredness of those who hold it. The spiritual discipline of attempting to read the Bible in the heart and mind of Jesus, not just in the heart and mind of our intellect and opinions; upholds the sacredness of scripture and empowers our reading.

Jesus often taught using parables. The parables were stories about people's reactions and behaviors within everyday circumstances and events. Each story revealed a deep truth about the human condition. To argue about whether or not these stories are historically true would be to absurdly disengage ourselves from their meaning. The foundational purpose of the Bible is the transmission of truth that we can live by.

Within the Bible we witness the timeless love of the lifeforce woven through all creation, a presence that is life itself. The Bible guides us in our living within the mystery of this eternal connection moment by moment.

A spiritual awakening is bringing people back to the Bible. The return awakens us to the beauty, wisdom and revelation that can be found within each book of each testament.

How we come to the Bible is critical. If we come looking only to justify our beliefs, little will occur within us beyond a cementing of our self-centered fear-filled belief systems. But if we go to the Bible with our human spirits open and a willingness to embrace the Spirit of the lifeforce that guided the hearts and minds of those who recorded these timeless revelations, our lives can be transformed.

The Bible invites us to open ourselves to the wondrous mystery of the eternal web of connection we are held within. If we can get over what the Bible isn't, we have an opportunity to receive what it is; a path to redemption, hope and peace.

Applying the Encounter to Our Lives

- Consider your relationship to the Bible. What (if anything) does the Bible mean to you?

- Has something or someone turned you off to the Bible?

- How is the Bible not true?

- How is the Bible true?

- Do you have a favorite Bible story, or favorite book of the Bible? Explain why you are drawn to the story or book.

- Is the Bible holy? If the Bible is holy, how is it holy? If the Bible is not holy, why is it not holy?

Read the parable of the Prodigal Son *(Luke 15:11-32)*. What do you think this parable is trying to say? Does it have more than one meaning? What character in the story do you most relate to? Did the story related in this parable actually happen in real life?

Meditation Exercise

The Bible has been handed down from generation to generation for thousands of years. Find a Bible and hold it in your hands, letting it comfortably rest on your lap as you sit. Set your timer to four minutes.

Meditate on the ancient writings that have been handed down to you. Try not to focus on anything but the giftedness of what now is passed to you. Receive the gift without judging or evaluating. This is what has been passed down. This will be a gift or curse or nothing depending on how you receive it. In these minutes focus only on receiving, on holding, holding what has been given.

Repeat this exercise daily until the next encounter.

5

Jesus, Firstborn of a New Humanity

Revolution

What Jesus began was nothing short of a revolution. Jesus was accused of sedition by the state, of blasphemy by the religious institution. He was executed as a revolutionary. The early Christian community that emerged after his death was accused of turning the whole world upside down.

Now, at this time in human history, two thousand years after its beginning, the revolution that Jesus began has become critical for human survival.

The teachings and life of Jesus demonstrate another way of living: simply, peacefully, together. To establish the new reign that Jesus envisioned and that the early community of Jesus began to put into practice, almost all of our belief systems must once again be turned upside down.

This encounter seeks to set the stage for the emergence of a new creation, of a new species of human beings; the spiritual rebirth of humanity.

Jesus is to be the firstborn
Of many children of the lifeforce.
From: Romans 8:28

If anyone is in Christ, they have become
A new creature; the old system has passed
Away; behold new things have come.
From: 2 Corinthians 5:17

Those who received Him were empowered to
Become children of the lifeforce, not born from
flesh and blood through sexual union but from
the power of the lifeforce.

From: John 1:12-13

The one who believes in me, will not only do
the works that I do, but even greater works
because I go to the lifeforce.

From: John 14:12

The Mission

The mission of Jesus is to bring humanity into a conscious daily relationship with the lifeforce. Jesus is the prototype for a new humanity. He introduces a new way of being alive, a new reign that would counter the mindset, values, economics, and violence of the world's existing kingdoms.

This new way of being could *NOT* be realized simply by establishing new enlightened understandings that would reform old systems. What Jesus sought for us was a conscious moment by moment connection to the lifeforce. Unifying with the lifeforce necessitated a dissolving of our union with systems that have become prisons of separation.

Jesus' deep intimate connection to the lifeforce is possible for us:

May they all be one,
Just as I am in the lifeforce,
And the lifeforce is in me,
May they be united in us.

Jesus, from John 17:21

Jesus Is Not God

Jesus is not God. Jesus did not come to establish a new religion. The new religion, Christianity, which developed after Jesus, made Jesus a God to excuse its leaders and practitioners from participating in the new life Jesus ordained.

The implication is clear: if Jesus is God you can't be expected to be like him.

Jesus is the Christ, the anointed one of the lifeforce, the firstborn of a new humanity that is emerging to transform the world into a new creation.

The Religionists' Creed

The Apostle's Creed, an early foundational document of an increasingly institutionalized Christianity focuses not on who we are in Christ or who we are becoming but on what we believe. The Apostle's Creed still reflects the foundational belief system of the institution of the church.

The Apostles Creed

I believe in God,
the Father almighty,
Creator of heaven and earth,
and in Jesus Christ, his only Son, our Lord,
who was conceived by the Holy Spirit,
born of the Virgin Mary,
suffered under Pontius Pilate,
was crucified, died and was buried;
he descended into hell;
on the third day he rose again from the dead;
he ascended into heaven,
and is seated at the right hand of God the Father almighty;
from there he will come to judge the living and the dead.
I believe in the Holy Spirit,
the holy catholic Church,
the communion of saints,
the forgiveness of sins,
the resurrection of the body,
and life everlasting. Amen.

Christianity came to focus on believing in Jesus over and against entering into the totality of being alive within the lifeforce that Jesus taught, demonstrated and died for. The Apostles Creed eliminates the life of Jesus. It goes from "born of the virgin Mary" to "suffered under Pontius Pilate, was crucified, dead, and buried". The Apostles creed sets the course for an afterlife, heaven focused religion. The functionaries of this new religion gained increasing power. They determined who was going to heaven and who was going to hell. Christianity began to grow further and further away from the purpose, life, teaching and empowering presence of Jesus.

Jesus became the God that if you believed in, in the right way, you would go to heaven. The more Jesus was worshipped, the less he was followed.

Gospel

The first four books of the New Testament tell the story of Jesus' life. The books are called the Gospels of Matthew, Mark, Luke and John. The Gospel of Mark is the earliest, written approximately 50 years after the death and resurrection of Jesus. This earliest Gospel does not begin with the birth of Jesus as do the Gospels of Matthew and Luke. Mark begins with the rebirth of Jesus. Jesus goes to the Jordan River to be baptized by John the Baptist. Jesus emerges from the water a new creation, the Christ. The Holy Spirit hovers over the water and over Jesus. The Spirit then accompanies him into the wilderness to confront temptation that could sever his connection to the lifeforce. We will return to this theme of rebirth in Encounter 6.

The gospels of Matthew and Luke begin with birth stories that establish Jesus' divinity. In these accounts Jesus isn't born like the rest of us, from a sexual union between a man and a woman.

In Jesus' case God impregnates a woman through a union with the Holy Spirit. Just so there are no questions we are assured that the woman, Mary the mother of Jesus, is a virgin.

Being born of a virgin was a fairly common theme of the times to designate the divine specialness of an emperor. Obeying the emperor became analogous with obeying God. As Christianity became increasingly religionized, the king like divinity and separateness of Jesus became more entrenched.

Diminishing the humanity of Jesus diminishes the significance of his life and the life he intends for us. We are taken off the hook related to his purpose. Jesus after all isn't like us, he's divine.

Religion has also deemed Mary, the mother of Jesus, to be divine. She is seen as pure because she doesn't debase herself by having sex to get pregnant. Mary is deified more for her virginity than her faith.

Diminishing Mary's humanity is a form of disrespect. Mary's courage, faith and transformation are too often disregarded. Worshipping Mary is a way to dismiss her. Her life should be emulated not worshipped.

Parable

And yet, the birth story is a beautiful parable of the new realm that Jesus sets in motion. Here is a king that exposes the emptiness and ultimate powerlessness of all the world's kings and their kingdoms. Here is a king not born within a palace but a stable. Here is a king whose parents aren't royalty but live on the edge of poverty. Here is a king without a sword who stands with the outcasts and powerless. Here is a king whose power causes empires to tremble.

The Second Birth

With all that the story of the birth of Jesus symbolizes, the primary birth in the life of Jesus and in our own lives occurs within the second birth. Jesus is the firstborn of a new humanity and this birth does not occur for him or for us when we come into the world from our mother's body. We are not first and foremost the children of our biological parents.

Those who received him were empowered to
become children of the lifeforce, not born from
flesh and blood through sexual union but from
the power of the lifeforce.
From: John 1:12

Jesus is born of the lifeforce and that birth is available to us. He is the first-born, the prototype, the teacher, the master, the empowerer, the anointed one, the Christ, the birth of spiritual awakening.

INVENTIONS

One of the most significant things that human beings have ever done was to create God in their own image in their own image they created him a sixty-ish white haired bearded superman with white flowing robes who speaks in a deep masculine voice and created the world in six days making the earth the moon the sun the water fashioning mountains trees birds animals dinosaurs insects a man out of clay then so the man wouldn't be lonely taking a rib from his body and forming a woman to help the man and then on the seventh day resting because creating the universe is exhausting work but of course much more powerful than the actual Superman whose arch enemy is Lex Luthor while God's is Satan who is a hundred times more powerful than Lex Luthor but only maybe fifty times more powerful than kryptonite and God hates bad people who don't worship him in the right way and gets jealous and angry if people worship someone other than him sending them to hell to burn forever but loves the group who worships him right and sends them to heaven forever while the second most amazing thing that humans do is take a man who is so deeply connected to the lifeforce that he embodies love that connects every created thing and they make him a God because we can't be expected to be like that and if we were what would happen to our churches and pastors and priests and bishops and the rich and powerful and who would even want their child to grow up to be president under those conditions and we probably could no longer be a republican or democrat or evangelical or liberal or conservative or fundamentalist or progressive because it would no longer make us feel special because we would just love everyone and not kill anyone or hate anyone or rob anyone or lie or steal or be entertained by TV shows or movies or games where people shoot one another or murder the beautiful young woman because it would no longer make us feel good to see that kind of thing and so much of what we are about would be lost that nothing would be the same and we would no longer feel like we needed to be in control or more important than other people or any other created thing but that we were a part of every created thing and it might feel weird at first to have love getting in the way of destroying our enemies or a fetus maybe really is a human being or using someone only for our pleasure would no longer give us pleasure and perhaps Jesus really was just a man well maybe not just a man but the first of a new species of human being and it could be different if we started living the way he did connected to the lifeforce and stopped being afraid and began to change into a new species as maybe he was saying all along and evolve a second time from being homo sapien into becoming home spiritus and as we left the water this time it would actually feel like we were being born again.

Applying the Encounter to Our Lives

- How might the world change if it adapted to the life and teachings of Jesus? Try to be specific, considering nations, states, towns, neighborhoods, economic, and social justice.

- How might your life change if you adapted to the life and teachings of Jesus. Try to be specific.

- How is spiritual awakening tied to the development of a new humanity?

- How is spiritual awakening different from just trying to be better people?

- Do you agree that religion often blocks spiritual awakening?

- Can the institutions of religion survive a spiritual awakening?

- How is Jesus the "firstborn of a new humanity"?

- How might a focus on Jesus get in the way of a spiritual awakening?

- Consider what is happening in the world at this time. How might a true spiritual revolution speak to the issues of racism, terrorism, the increasing power of the rich, poverty, environmental degradation, globalization, war?

Meditation Exercise

In our fast paced, constantly moving, technologically connected world, sitting in meditation without our minds continuing to race is an extremely difficult task. Progress is going to be slow. We are addicted to our pace. Freeing ourselves from addiction occurs one small step at a time.

Set your timer for five minutes. Before you begin consider your addiction, your addictive pace, your addictive thinking. Be aware of how difficult it is to stop for five minutes.

Do you feel anxious as you prepare to start the timer? Do you believe that something new can happen in your life? Consider the price of spiritual awakening, all that might have to change. It begins with stopping.

Start the timer. For the next five minutes live within the first stages of awakening. Give yourself to being at peace. If you lose your concentration give yourself to laughter. Laugh at the difficulty of resting your mind for five minutes, laugh at yourself, then focus on each breath you take, return to peace.

Repeat this exercise daily until the next encounter.

A New Creation

The Waters

The very first two verses of Genesis, the very first two verses of the Bible, point us toward a profound spiritual revelation of creation that links to the biological formation of all life on Earth.

> *And the earth was formless and*
> *void, and darkness was over the surface*
> *of the deep; and the Spirit of the lifeforce*
> *was moving over the surface of*
> *the waters.*
>
> *From: Genesis 1:1-2*

As the Spirit hovered over the waters, the sea covered earth became a womb from which life on Earth would emerge. The concentration of salt within the ocean is nearly the same as the concentration of salt within the waters of a mother's womb.

In our primal physical beginning we came from the sea and we came forth as we are now from the dark, wet, warm sea of our mother's body.

As human beings, we are deeply linked to water, 60% of our body mass is water, and our bodies demand a daily intake of water to function properly. Beyond our physical needs we are drawn to water for reasons that lie deep within us. We continually seek the water's edge, we are drawn to a connecting force beyond simple reason, pulled by something deep within us, something that touches the origins of our physical and spiritual being. The sounds, smell, the taste of the sea link us to our beginnings.

> *Jesus answered, Truly, Truly, I say to you, unless one is born of water and the Spirit, that person can never enter the realm of the lifeforce. From: John 3:5.*

To grasp our connection to water and Spirit is to grasp an essential connection to creator and creation. We are part of something larger and deeper than we can name or fully comprehend, but even as we begin to identify our longing, the journey back to a unified beginning of water and Spirit starts to reshape our lives in the present, and we are drawn toward a life giving future. This is the beginning of our awakening.

Prior to the beginning of his public ministry, Jesus journeyed to the Jordan River to be baptized by John the Baptist. The Jordan River, strung between the Dead Sea and the Sea of Galilee, becomes the birth canal for the first-born of a new species. John had been baptizing in water for repentance in preparation for what would soon emerge. He spoke of the one coming . . . .

> *"I baptize you with water for repentance, but one who is more powerful than I is coming after me. He will baptize you with the Holy Spirit and fire." From Matthew 3:11, NASB.*

As He ascended from the water, the Holy Spirit, in the form of a dove, hovered again over the waters.

> *After being baptized, Jesus went up immediately from the water; and behold, the heavens were opened, and he saw the Spirit of the lifeforce descending as a dove, and coming upon Him, and behold a voice out of the heavens saying, This is my beloved son in whom I am well pleased. From: Matthew 3:16-17.*

Following the baptism, Jesus walked into the wilderness accompanied by the Holy Spirit to spend forty days fasting in preparation for all that he would encounter on his journey to bring humanity into a new realm of consciousness. In the wilderness Jesus confronted all that would separate him from living within the new realm. Jesus, himself, was tempted to cling to the values of a realm that would need to pass away.

The Followers of Jesus

Following his ministry on Earth, his death and resurrection, Jesus instructed his followers to go to Jerusalem where they would receive the Holy Spirit. As Jesus ascends from the earthly to the heavenly realm a new possibility of connection to the lifeforce is released. Jesus will be more fully present to his followers following his earthly separation from them.

> "I will not leave you as orphans; I will come to you. After a little while the world will behold me no more; but you will behold me, because I live, you shall live also. In that day you shall know that I am in my Father, and you in me and I in you." From John 14:18-20, NASB.

After receiving the Holy Spirit, the followers of Jesus immediately begin offering the experience to all they encounter.

> And Peter said to them, "Repent and let each of you be baptized in the name of Jesus Christ, releasing you from the imprisonment of your separation, and you shall receive the gift of the Holy Spirit. From: Acts 2:38.

The early followers of Jesus were immersed in water and emerged born anew, baptized in water and baptized in the Holy Spirit; baptized into a new way of being alive, a new and ancient realm recognized almost immediately as the source of the great river from which all life flows out. The lifeforce flows out in creation, Christ flows out upon the world, the Spirit flows out upon humanity. Baptized in the Holy Spirit the followers of Jesus now immersed in the lifeforce enter the flowing current of love that moves through all created things.

We Are Known, We Belong

Before they were called Christians followers of Jesus were called followers of "The Way". Baptism represented a form of dying and emerging from the water into a new way of being alive. As our human ancestors emerged from the water within the first creation on Earth, our spiritual ancestors emerged from water into a new creation. Baptism represented a form of dying, an end of the old self, and an emerging from the water into a new way of being alive.

"Therefore if any person is in Christ, they are a new creature; the old things have passed away, behold new things have come." 2 Corinthians 5:17, NASB.

In this transformation through the Holy Spirit a new connection to the lifeforce and all creation begins, a connection that had been severed in the Garden when man and woman fell away from union.

Within this death of the old self, the Adam self, the Eve self, there is a resurrection into a new primal self, from the water emerges a new species. The new species is not solely an earthly creation but a new creature, whose origins in Christ are prior to the creation of Earth, prior to the creation of the universe.

"I have been crucified with Christ; and it is no longer I who live, but Christ lives in me." Galatians 2:20a, NASB.

In our union with Christ we become children of the lifeforce and our origins reach back through Christ prior to creation.

For He is the image of the lifeforce; the firstborn of all creation; for in Him all things in Heaven and on Earth were created. From: Colossians 1:15.

Jesus becomes the prototype, the firstborn of what is to become a new species of humanity.

We are known before time, destined to be conformed to the image of the son, that he might be the firstborn of many daughters and sons. From: Romans 8:29.

We have been known, connected to the lifeforce before time began. As we receive the Holy Spirit we recognize that we have always felt this connection from a deep place within our spirits. This familiar place is for the first time recognized, for the first time known; this is our home, we have come home.

Life is restored to us, the unity of our belonging is restored; loss has become gain, emptiness has become fullness, enemies have become friends, death has become life.

Applying the Encounter to Our Lives

- Consider your own connection to water. What waters have you been drawn to through your life? Are there lakes, ponds, streams, rivers, oceans that hold a special meaning?

- Think about how your experiences around water varied in different seasons of your life; through childhood, teen years, young adult, middle age and older years.

- How are baptism and rebirth linked?

- Jesus must have been around the age of thirty when he went to John to be baptized. This baptism preceded his public ministry. Consider what this baptism was about.

- In this lesson receiving the Holy Spirit is connected to baptism. Consider why this connection may be significant.

Meditation Exercise

Consider for a moment your first nine months of life within your mother's womb. Think about those months of growth and development from a microscopic gathering of cells to a baby ready for birth, as a metaphor for spiritual rebirth. For nine months you were being held and sustained within your Mother's body until you were ready to emerge.

Think now about how you are held and sustained within the atmosphere, the womb of the Earths body. Think now about being held and sustained eternally by the invisible web of the lifeforce.

Set the timer for six minutes. Meditate on being held and sustained through these minutes. Do not think about being held and sustained, enter a state of being held and sustained. Be held and sustained within these six minutes.

Repeat this exercise daily until the next encounter.

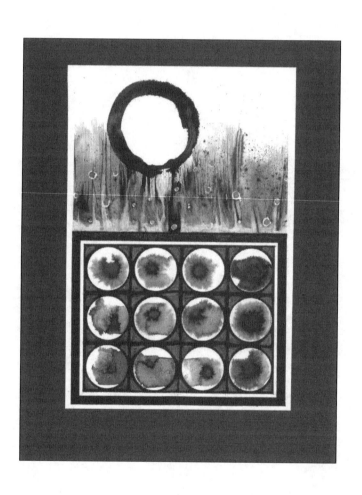

A New Community

From the Ruins

The institution of the church will continue to crumble under the weight of its programs, property and professional clergy. Most North American churches are being kept afloat financially by people over sixty. The church as we know it is also crumbling under the weight of belief systems that are clung to in order to perpetuate the power of a few and the delusion of the many. We have passed through a time in which the foundation of religion was based on what people believed. We are entering a time in which faith is determined by how one lives out what they believe.

The debris of the crumbling religious landscape is being cleared away for the emerging community of Jesus. What these communities will look like remains unclear. It is however likely that building-centered, Sunday-centered, clergy-centered, program- centered, empire-centered Christianity has seen its day.

The emerging community of Jesus may look similar to the church in its earliest beginnings. Small groups of people will begin meeting in homes. There will be no paid clergy. As soon as someone is paid, it becomes difficult not to protect one's job and the institution that provides it.

Success will not be measured in numbers, or buildings, or programs, or finances, or dynamic leaders but upon the depth, love, faith and walk of the community.

Twelve members cannot sustain the program, building, and clergy of an institutional church. Twelve people committed together to the life that Jesus demonstrated and empowered can begin to turn the world upside down.

The community's focus will be upon continually growing into the depths of the lifeforce. As one grows in spiritual maturity, an ever-increasing humility develops. Our spiritual eyes are opened to greater depths that arise before us. We become both thankful for what is emerging within us and humbled by the vastness of the depths yet to be discovered and embraced.

A new form of monasticism, of the shared life within community is emerging within the awakening. Within this monastic model of the shared life the varied gifts and ministries of each member of the community become identified and supported. There will be teachers, administrators, pastors, artists, musicians, prophets, poets, healers, craftspeople; and the list goes on.

The community will continually search for ways to be less dependent on a culture of consumption. Racial and gender equality will be intentionally embraced.

Those with greater financial means will not be given more voice or power within the community than those with little means.

Those who are often considered outsiders within the culture will be welcomed, cared for, and included. Sexual orientation will not limit or enhance one's place within the community. All sexual orientations will hold the expression of their sexuality under the light of Jesus.

Liturgies of connection will be developed and will change as the depth of our connection grows.

Music will no longer be used as filler within a service of worship. Music will flow out of the depths and longings of the community. No particular forms or expressions of music will be given legitimacy over and against other forms and expressions.

The arts will be employed to express the spiritual insights of the community. Poetry, painting, pottery, sculpture, printmaking, writing, drawing and filmmaking will be understood as expressions within spiritual awakening.

Although the culture often displays an addictive relationship to technology, technology will be employed in a discerning manner within community.

Attachments to cell phones often appear to be addictive. There is a growing need to be continually attached through many forms of technology. While this may be doing damage to our spirits and be a limited means of connection, it may also be an attempt to fill our emptiness, to satisfy a deep desire to make real and lasting connections. The cell phone and ever increasing social media avenues of connection reveal our deepest desires. The possibility for true spiritual awakening is growing because of technology's ultimate limitations.

We will begin to learn how to stay continually and deeply connected through the web flowing from the lifeforce through the cosmos.

The community of Jesus does not gather around its rightness or goodness, but around its need. Our weakness and our strength will be exposed. We are in this together; we all suffer from our own forms of crippling addictions. Knowing this we come together in humble acceptance of ourselves and each other. Those who naively believe in their own strength and rightness can do great damage to the community. Humility is a by-product of spiritual awakening and an essential ingredient of community.

Core Values

As a spiritually awakened group of people continue to meet, their life together often grows more intentional. The development of core values can be a way of unifying the group, of clarifying its purpose for being.

This lesson concludes with the core values of the A Place Apart community. These are included to give you a starting point as you consider your own core values.

Core Values of A Place Apart

A Place Apart's core values are those aspects of our faith and life which bind us together as a community and that allow us to build together. Our covenant to live and work together includes a commitment to live and work within these core values. These Core Values are not meant to be a statement of doctrine, nor do they enumerate all of our concerns and interests. Rather, they describe what is unique about A Place Apart, and what commitments are central to our being.

A Prayer for A Place Apart

The Prayer goes hand-in-hand with the core values of A Place Apart. A Place Apart is not a place of stagnant doctrine nor formulaic statements of purpose. It is a place of constant, fervent prayer. The Prayer is a humble and earnest plea for new life. It is also a reminder of the values that the participants in A Place Apart have covenanted to live by. Instead of "Amen" we now allow the day to put feet upon our prayer; our life begins to become an extension of our prayers.

Core Values of A Place Apart

I

We commit ourselves to total participation in a new way of living, a new way of being fully alive introduced by Jesus Christ, made possible through his life, death, resurrection and ascension and empowered by the Holy Spirit. (*Luke 17:20-21*)

> Holy presence,
>
> May your new reign come.
>
> Bless us and commit us totally to that new reign,
>
> And to the new way of living introduced by Jesus Christ and empowered
>
> By your Holy Spirit.

II

We commit ourselves to developing covenant community within which all types of people can live and work together, for longer and shorter periods of time, to live into the new way of being fully alive which Jesus described as the lifeforce.

> Blessed presence,
>
> May your will be done on earth as it is in heaven.
>
> And on this earth, anoint us to live together as a covenant community of your people.
>
> May our hearts be open to welcome visitors of any race, any creed, any tribe, just as Christ welcomes us.

III

We commit ourselves to developing a new relationship to the created order of the lifeforce, to live daily within the rhythms of that order with an understanding of the web of connection present within every aspect of creation.

> Revealing presence,
>
> Give us today our daily bread,
>
> And set us free with the knowledge that all our needs are met by the earth.
>
> Renew our relationship with your created order,
>
> Guide us through the natural rhythms of life,
>
> And reveal yourself to us
>
> In every drop of dew,
>
> Every blade of grass,
>
> Every crumb of bread.
>
> Convict us with the knowledge that all creation is made sacred through Christ.

IV

We commit ourselves to honoring scripture as the word of the lifeforce, revealed wholly in Jesus, the word made flesh. The gospel message (new life), and the gospel medium (new people), are one.

Beautiful presence

And beautiful is Jesus Christ, the word,

Revealed to us through the words of scripture.

Illuminate our understanding of the testaments,

So that the gospel message—new life—

And the gospel medium—new people—

May be one.

V

We commit ourselves to Christ-like hospitality and teaching. We are a teaching community, understanding that the daily rhythms of our life together in Christ will be our primary teaching, and that welcoming others into those rhythms will be our means of prophetic witness.

Loving presence

You welcome in the weary travelers on life's long road.

Send us your loving Spirit,

So that we too may be good innkeepers

To our fellow travelers on the journey.

VI

We commit ourselves to participate in lifestyles of peace, non-violence, and justice for the sake of the world and for the healing and health of our own souls. We understand that to some extent none of us can be free to be fully alive until all are free to be so.

Just presence

You bless the meek and call the peacemakers your children.

Empower us with strength to work for justice,

To live peaceably with one another within your world,

So that even the least of us can live in freedom and fullness of life.

VII

We commit ourselves to periodically examine our individual lives and our life together in light of what we have claimed to be our core values.

> Merciful presence
>
> Forgive us our sins, as we forgive those who sin against us.
>
> Make us mindful that there is always more to learn,
>
> And a deeper understanding to be gained
>
> Through reflection and reevaluation of our life together.
>
> May this prayer strike our hearts anew this day,
>
> And every day.

Applying the Encounter to Our Lives

- What makes a community a community?

- What makes a community a community of Jesus?

- What might be lost or gained if Christianity as we have known it began to disappear? What might be the effect of fewer church buildings, fewer clergy, fewer programs, fewer services, fewer Christians?

- Imagine the community of Jesus in the future. What might it look like? What would you want it to be?

- How might the arts be important within community?

- In what ways might traditional understandings of failure and success be different within a new community of Jesus.

- Look over each of A Place Apart's Core Values. Are there any you question? Are there any that you would add?

- If you are using this guide within a group, how is your group a community? How is it not a community?

- Where do you find your primary community?

- Why is humility an essential ingredient of community?

Meditation Exercise

Set your timer to seven minutes. You have been surrounded your entire life by a "cloud of witnesses" (*Hebrews 11:32-12:2a*); by great numbers of people who were both here before your life began and with you during your life; people who have sacrificed, built, prepared the way for you and cared for you and loved you. Close your eyes and let the faces of your community past and present appear before you. Do not spend time evaluating or judging their effect on you, just see them with the eyes of your heart. Allow one to come after another and let your spirit be touched as it will.

Start the timer. Give yourself to the Spirit beyond yourself.

Repeat this exercise daily until the next encounter.

Out of the Shadows

Mary Magdalene and the Presence of Women

Out of the Shadows

Many women were there, looking on. They had followed Jesus from Galilee and had provided for him. Among them were his mother and his mother's sister, and Mary Magdalene. Matthew 27:55-56, NASB.

From the beginning women were present in a remarkable way at every juncture of Jesus' ministry. They go with him into Jerusalem; they are present at the crucifixion and are the first to experience the resurrection. All four gospels reveal that women are the first to give testimony of the risen Christ. In this respect, they are the first evangelists. Following his crucifixion, death and resurrection, Jesus appeared to his followers just prior to his ascension. He told them of an upper room in Jerusalem where they were to go and wait for the empowering presence of the Holy Spirit.

These things I have spoken to you, while abiding with you. But the Helper, the Holy Spirit, whom the lifeforce will send in my name, will teach you all things, and help you to remember all that I said to you. From: John 14: 25-26.

Over a hundred women and men met together and waited together to receive what had been promised. Each one of them experienced a life changing indwelling of the Holy Spirit. The community of Jesus, women and men together, was born within that gathering.

Jesus' respect for and inclusion of women radically contrasts with and confronts the culture and religious establishment of his day.

Tragically, two thousand years later, Jesus' respect for and inclusion of women contrasts radically with and confronts the culture and religious establishment of our day.

Each of the four major world religions; Christianity, Judaism, Islam and Buddhism have been dominated by men. Historically women are regarded as religions second-class citizens. Participation in religion is limited to keeping "them" in "their place." Traditionally males have occupied all positions of leadership and decision-making. Complete male domination only began to somewhat erode within some branches of some religions through the 20th century.

The subservient role of women is perhaps most tragic within Christianity. Rejecting the full inclusion of women within the Christian community can be seen as a betrayal of its founder. In the early church women had been granted a status with the Christian community that they had never experienced in their religion or culture. This stature had clearly been granted and modeled by Jesus. Jesus' relationship to and inclusion of women was a confrontation of the religious, and political culture of the day.

Shadows Re-emerge

Women clearly felt a transforming and liberating inclusion following the death and resurrection of Jesus and throughout the early formation of the Christian faith. Women could freely join in worship with men, they could speak within community gatherings. Their heads no longer needed to be covered. There existed a new reality in all relationships within this emerging community of sisters and brothers.

The tragedy, of course, is that this liberation of role, of one's place and spirit did not last for women. Men's historically dominant roles were being threatened. As the early church became more institutionalized, women began to lose their equal place.

Women were forbidden to speak when the church assembled. No doubt there had been times within their early liberation when women did not share thoughtfully. This, no doubt, felt shocking within their culture; that women would actually speak their mind without caution.

The unthoughtful sharing of men would, of course, not be held to the same standard. The unshackling that women suddenly felt through their relationship to the risen Christ was again deemed by men; against the way the world had been established by God from the beginning.

Women were silenced. They were told to cover their heads. The scandal of their liberation was ended, as was the scandal of the cross, as was the scandal of Jesus' relationship to women.

It was not just through the institutionalization of the Christian religion and its subsequent marriage to empire 300 years after its beginning that the way, truth and life of Jesus became lost. The community of Jesus stepped into lostness when women's voices, women's full participation and women's spirits were shackled.

We continue to live within a world in which women are denied adequate health care and education and in which women are murdered, beaten, raped, enslaved and impoverished.

As women around the world continue to live under varying degrees of injustice and oppression, the stark reality is that half of the human family routinely experiences injustice.

While complete liberation of women in all aspects of civic and religious life is a social justice issue, for the sake of the fullness of human life on Earth it is foundationally a quality of human life issue. The community of Jesus will not be established on Earth as it is in Heaven until women are unshackled within local communities and throughout the Earth.

Mary Magdalene

While Jesus demonstrated a radical inclusion of women in general, his relationship to one woman; Mary Magdalene, is significant. As the early church became an increasingly male dominated institution, the primary role that women played throughout the life and ministry of Jesus was covered over. Mary Magdalene was a disciple of Jesus, as were many women who were following him around the countryside as he taught. Mary called him "Teacher".

In what was nothing less than a smear campaign, Mary Magdalene was referred to as a prostitute and her role within the life of Jesus and the new community that emerged after Jesus was all but erased.

It is only through ancient writings about the life of Jesus, discovered in the last century, that a new (ancient) view of Mary Magdalene is emerging.

There is obviously much about Mary Magdalene (and about Jesus) that we will never know. The depth of their relationship is made clear in the Bible. How that relationship functioned in their life together is not clear.

Is it possible that Jesus and Mary Magdalene were married? Why might the very idea of Jesus being married be offensive or faith shaking to anyone? It would have been unusual for a man at that time in that culture not to be married. It is reasonable to assume that the male disciples of Jesus were married. There is a brief Biblical reference supporting this likelihood.

Peter's mother in-law had grown ill and during a visit Jesus healed her. Without this one incident we would not know that any of the disciples were married. This short account leads us to assume they were.

The tremendous influence that the apostle Paul had within the early church and his views on women, marriage and sexuality held great sway in the formation of the Christian religion.

To this day the birth of Jesus through a virgin continues to be a cornerstone of religious belief. Many religious leaders still promote the life-long virginity of Mary the mother of Jesus despite the appearance of the siblings of Jesus throughout the gospels. This kind of denial exposes a low view of marriage and cements an understanding that this coming together is somehow tainted by sexual union. The idea that to not marry and to commit to celibacy is a higher calling perpetuates views of marriage and sexuality that separate us from the lifeforce, the Earth and all its beings.

How different might the world have been the last 2,000 years if it was known that Jesus was married and had children. Would the teachings of Jesus, his sacrifice, death and resurrection be any less meaningful?

The vision of Jesus and Mary Magdalene united in body, mind and spirit; partners in life and ministry, might have changed the way women were regarded and been a model for the union that is to be at the foundation of marriage.

Again A Garden

Married or not, Mary Magdalene and Jesus were united in their spirits. The depths of their bond was revealed in Mary's encounter with Jesus at the tomb in the garden. The disciples, Peter and John, had come to the tomb, found it empty and gone back home.

Mary lingers outside the tomb weeping. She turns around and Jesus is standing near her but she does not recognize him. Jesus asks her "Woman, why are you weeping." Still not recognizing and thinking that he is the gardener, she asks where the body has been taken. At this point Jesus speaks one word, "Mary". At the speaking of her name she sees him. Mary responds with one word, "Teacher".

Mary embraces Jesus and he tells her that she can no longer cling to him and must now go and tell his followers what his rising from the dead means. She runs from the garden and the empty tomb and is the first to tell of the meaning of his resurrection.

In Genesis, the first book of the Bible, in its first three chapters man and woman are created in a garden. They act in a way that separates them from God and one another and the creation's order. Man and woman experience shame and seek to cover over their nakedness. They are expelled from the garden and their descendants continue to live in separation. This separation is equated to death and this is the human story.

This lineage of separation is broken when Mary Magdalene enters another garden looking for the dead body of the one she loves and finds him alive. The embrace of Jesus and Mary ends the lineage of the curse of separation between woman and man and all creation. She runs from the garden ALIVE!

Applying the Encounter to Our Lives

- If you are sitting in a circle, go around the circle, giving each woman present an opportunity to share experiences within their lives in which they felt diminished and disrespected as woman.

  NOTE: The group should understand that some women will not be able to share within the group, at this time, instances of devastating abuse and injustice.

- How has religion been a hindrance to the full liberation of women within society? How has religion been a promoter of the full liberation of women within society?

- For those who are a part of a religious community, how has your community changed over the years in its relationship to women? Are there examples of changes that remain to be made?

- What social justice issues related specifically to women need to be addressed in your town city state, and country?

- Do women receive the same level of health care as men?

- Who was Mary Magdalene and what does her life, so much as we know, reveal to us? The following references to Mary Magdalene can be found in the New Testament:

  Luke 8:1-3   Luke 7:40-50   Luke 10:38-42   John 11:1-40

  John 12:1-8   John 19:25   John 20:11-18   Matthew 27:55

  The following references are called apocryphal, writings from the New Testament period discovered in the 20th century:

  Philip 61:32, 65:55, 66:60, 72, 76

  Mary 8: 15-24, 9:1-20, 10:4-25, 17:1-20

- What is the role of sexuality in those seeking to live within the way, truth, and life of Jesus?

- How is Mary Magdalene speaking to us in this age?

Meditation Exercise

Set your timer to eight minutes. Sit comfortably in a quiet place. Allow Mary Magdalene to enter your conscious and unconscious mind. Allow Mary Magdalene's presence to be present within your spirit. Let the presence of Mary Magdalene anoint your body, mind and spirit. Allow her to comfort you. Her presence will reveal to you what you need to hear. In silence she will speak directly to your heart, your spirit and soul.

Repeat this exercise daily until the next encounter.

Introduction to Warrior Mystic Monk

These encounters are designed to help you tap into, develop and nurture the raw innermost elements of your being; resident longings of your soul that may have been knocking on the door of your consciousness for years.

This encounter and the three following encounters seek to walk you into a new intentionality within the physical (warrior), spiritual (mystic) and relational (monk) aspects of your life.

We believe that within the warrior, within the mystic, within the monk reside a combination of foundational elements necessary to our wholeness.

To bring about a newness to being alive involves both a walking toward that which gives life fullness and a walking away from that which diminishes life.

Reaching for wholeness

Warriors, Mystics, and Monks are archetypal symbols that keep showing up throughout human history. They conjure up much more than vocational descriptions for soldiers, poets, and clerics. These are mythological archetypes that emerge in remarkably similar presentations from ancient times to the present; from Gilgamesh, to Star Wars, from Beowulf to The Lord of the rings.

Warrior, Mystic, Monk themes continually re-emerge, speaking to essential aspects of our humanness, our longing and belonging.

We are beginning to understand that within the structured, systematized culture of North America something raw and deep, something central to

73

our humanity, has been lost. Our humanity defies labeling as Republican, Democrat, conservative, liberal, left, right, religious, secular. We are beginning to understand that we desperately long for something that we cannot buy, something we cannot quite name, not quite define, nor see.

Warrior, Mystic, Monk; the lion, the tin man, the scarecrow in the land of Oz; the dwarfs, the elves, the hobbits of Tolkien's Middle Earth, the Celtic spirituality of the ancient druids that identified three circles of connection; the personal, the spiritual and the communal along with the Christian Holy Trinity, all contribute to a balance of understanding of our lives and the unified essence of the lifeforce.

George Lucas' Jedi understood the critical union of warrior-mystic-monk to their wholeness; lose one aspect and the Dark Side of the Force begins to take over.

When these central elements of our humanity are not acknowledged they cannot be understood, nor positively incorporated, nor held in proper perspective nor called forth to serve us.

So much consciously and unconsciously connects with us. We are drawn to this connectedness and our souls and spirits will not settle because our longing is so great. We don't even know how to name it, much less how to hold it.

Jesus, the Messiah, is sent into a messy world to save us , to reconcile our longings, to reconnect us to the lifeforce, to others, to the Earth and to ourselves. Jesus teaches and lives out the unifying principles of existence. His death unleashes "the Force"; the unifying elemental connectedness present at creation.

Although this union was lost in our rebellion against the created order of the lifeforce in the Garden, this connection remains our foundational legacy and our foundational longing.

Realizing our warrior-mystic-monk potential is central to our reconnecting to the life we were created for.

Jesus was essentially calling his followers to be warrior-mystic-monks for the sake of their own genuine aliveness and for the sake of the new reign of the lifeforce. Although our calling and our personal wiring may lead us to focus on a single designation, it is only in integrating these three aspects of being that we begin to find wholeness.

The warrior is one who rejects all forms of violence, but who prepares for spiritual battle through training, discipline, and strategy. The mystic is one who sees beyond the surface to see the lifeforce in all things, and who takes time to pray and commune with the lifeforce alone. The monk is a woman or a man, married or single, who lives a life of ordered devotion focusing especially on community, service, and hospitality.

Our spirits long for the fulfillment of what these designations signify. When the warrior aspects of our being, the mystic aspects of our being, the monk aspects of our being are not met and nurtured, great voids exist within our souls. We learn to cover over the empty places with philosophies, religious beliefs and behaviors that further separate us from the lifeforce, from one another, from creation and our essential selves.

Warrior Mystic Monks is not what we "should" be to be "good Christians," but what Jesus invites us to live into for the sake of our own wholeness.

As we live in the balance of the warrior mystic monk we begin to live within the rhythm of the heartbeat of all that the lifeforce has created.

Living As a Warrior Mystic Monk

We long to be whole but live within a culture that increasingly isolates us from creator and creation. The frantic pace and constant distractions of contemporary life separate us from knowing our innermost selves, from knowing and truly connecting with others. So much of what we seek and do plays into maintaining a consumer driven culture that demands we cover over our deepest longings. We structure our lives to minimize the pain of our emptiness.

As we prepare to step into the warrior, into the mystic, into the monk, we understand that we also begin to step away from a culture whose values and direction collide with the life we now seek.

We all possess some traits of warriors, mystics and monks. Most of us gravitate toward one or two of these designations because of our particular make up, the genes we have inherited, our upbringing, gifts and interests. Some of us are more naturally warriors, some more naturally mystics, some more naturally monks. The gifts and abilities we carry into life, the particular ways in which we are naturally wired tend to work for us and at times against us.

It is to be expected that we would embrace a way of life that comes naturally to us, that "fits", that compliments the way we are wired. It is also to be expected that we would steer clear of aspects of life that do not fit us so easily, areas in which we do not feel as gifted.

Jesus seems to have balanced aspects of all three designations. He is warrior, he is mystic, he is monk in equal portion. Throughout the New Testament Jesus draws on these aspects of being as the need arises.

We have come to believe that for one to be fully alive each of these aspects; warrior, mystic and monk, must be fully embraced. Uniting the warrior mystic monk within us unites us to the lifeforce and within that union we become whole.

In the next three lessons we will focus on the warrior (Encounter 10), on the mystic (Encounter 11), and on the monk (Encounter 12). We encourage you to engage each thoughtfully, but to especially focus upon those areas that do not come as naturally.

Spiritually awakened communities will be dependent upon each member striving to become a warrior mystic monk.

Stepping Toward Home: Searching for the Wizard

In the L. Frank Baum classic, The Wizard of Oz, the main character, a girl named Dorothy, finds herself exiled in an alien and dangerous land. She longs to find her way home. She is told that the all-powerful wizard of Oz holds the key to her return.

On her journey to Oz, she encounters a lion seeking courage (warrior), a tin man seeking a heart (mystic), and a scarecrow seeking a brain (monk). Embracing these three as "friends" will be critical to Dorothy finding her way home to her beloved Aunt Em.

When she arrives in the Emerald City of Oz, Dorothy discovers that the wizard's power to get her home in some magical way has been over-sold.

The wizard appears at first to be a fraud, the curtain that has hidden his identity is torn away and he seems only a weak human being.

When the separation is broken the wizard's true power is revealed. The wizard begins to awaken Dorothy, awaken the lion, awaken the tin man, awaken the scarecrow to the fact that they already possess what they seek.

The wizard offers Dorothy a ride back home on his hot air balloon but she misses this opportunity because she refuses to leave without her beloved dog Toto from whom she has been temporarily separated. The wizard's balloon sails off without her.

Dorothy travels with the lion, the tin man, and the scarecrow to the castle of the good witch Glenda. She asks Glenda to use her magical power to send her back home. Glenda reveals to Dorothy that she is already clothed with all the power she needs:

> *"Your silver shoes will carry you over the desert," replied Glenda. "If you had known their power you could have gone back to your Aunt Em the very first day you came to this country."*

> *"But then I should not have had my wonderful brains!" cried the Scarecrow. "I might have passed my whole life in the farmer's cornfield."*

> *"And I should not have had my lovely heart," said the tin Woodman. "I might have stood rusted in the forest till the end of the world."*

> *"And I should have lived a coward forever," declared the Lion, "and no beast in all the forest would have had a good word to say to me."*

> *"This is all true," said Dorothy, "and I am glad I was of use to these good friends. But now that each of them has had what he most desired, and each is happy in having a kingdom to rule besides, I think I should like to go back to Kansas."*

> *"The silver shoes," said the Good Witch, "have wonderful powers. And one of the most curious things about them is that they can carry you to anyplace in the world in three steps, and each step will be made in the wink of an eye. All you have to do is to knock the heels together three times and command the shoes to carry you wherever you wish to go."*

> *The Wizard of Oz* by L. Frank Baum

Trinity: The Three Within the One

The fullness of the lifeforce is revealed in three aspects of being, Parent, Child, and Holy Spirit.

In the beginning; God breathes all life into being, Christ is uniquely present as the Cosmos is formed, the Holy Spirit hovers over the waters of the emerging creation. So is each aspect of the lifeforce present as we become new creations; Warrior-Mystic-Monk emerge together, three steps away from an alien land and we are home.

Applying the Encounter to Our Lives

- Briefly try to describe your understandings of the warrior, of the mystic, of the monk. Remember that each of these designations will be the focus of the next three encounters.

- If you have seen the *Star Wars* films, think about how the Jedi incorporate the warrior mystic monk model.

- Do you believe that there are powers available to us beyond what we can normally see?

- Do you believe that there is a way of living, a way of being that could transform your life and the lives of all human beings?

- Is the Trinity; the one within the three; the lifeforce as parent, child, spirit; a way of describing the unifying mystery of our connection to the lifeforce?

Meditation Exercise

Set your timer to nine minutes. Consider the unity possible within the three; the warrior mystic monk; the unity within the three together that no single one can provide alone.

Meditate upon the three as one whole. Do not think about the attributes of each; we will be doing this in the next three encounters. Let your heart and spirit hold the three as one whole. Allow your spirit to receive the blessing of your own wholeness, as yet not fully known but now seen. You have begun to move toward this longed for union. Through the next nine minutes allow your spirit to bathe in the completeness of the warrior mystic monk.

Repeat this exercise daily until the next encounter.

Warrior

NOTE: The next three encounters are not simply informational, they are not presented just to teach you about warriors and mystics and monks. Each encounter is designed to help you enter into the warrior, mystic and monk way of life.

Becoming a Warrior

We must finally begin to understand what Jesus so clearly understood in his own life. We are in the midst of a battle that is continually being fought to win over our hearts and minds. Our thoughts, emotions and reactions are continually controlled by the battle that rages daily within and around us.

Either our warrior spirits will be nurtured for spiritual battle to be guided by the life affirming power of Christ or driven to destructive thinking and behaviors that war against our own wellbeing and the wellbeing of creation.

A warrior for the new reign introduced by Jesus is:

- One who rejects violence in any form.
- One who rejects the false, empty, temporal power of the world.
- One who understands the enduring power of self-giving love.
- One who is actively positioned against forces that destroy body, mind and spirit.

- One who sees the way of Jesus as the way of the warrior, as the model for warrior.

- One whose training and conditioning has prepared her to do battle intellectually, spiritually, physically.

- One who eats, drinks, exercises, trains and studies in preparation for all that will be encountered.

- One who develops a strategy for achieving new realm goals.

- One who is able to live in harsh conditions and under great pressure.

- One who is a protector of the weak, powerless and oppressed in the world.

- One who sees scripture as the warrior's training manual.

- One who loves her enemy, who returns violence, rejection, and hatred with love.

- One who understands the nature of the battle that is continually being waged, within and without to win our hearts and minds.

Warrior Exercises

Make a conscious decision to take responsibility for the care and development of your physical body. Consult your health care provider to work at a plan that is appropriate given your age, weight, and general physical condition. Do not seek quick results. Include both strength training and cardio-vascular training in your workout routine.

A few sessions with a qualified trainer or physical therapist is highly recommended. A trainer can maximize the effects of your workout and aid in minimizing vulnerability to injury as you are guided to work within your physical and emotional comfort zone.

The benefits of lifting weights for the development and maintenance of strong bones and muscle is being increasingly recommended for young and old alike.

Spend an hour outdoors each day. This time outside can also be used for cardio-vascular training.

The warrior is a defender and protector of the weak and powerless. The warrior works to empower the oppressed. Pray for discernment regarding the specifics of your social justice ministry.

Consider giving a significant period of time (a week, two weeks, forty days) to intensively preparing your body, mind and spirit to confront the principalities and powers that daily seek to own you.

Warriors are called to make sacrifices that will occasionally put their lives on the line. Write out arrangements for your funeral. Write out a will.

Seek to conquer your fears in all situations, especially the fear of what other people think of you. Pray for those who do not treat you well. Return evil with love. Remember, however, that casually accepting abusive treatment should not be considered loving.

Practice fearlessness by engaging in Christ-centered actions that demand you move beyond the security of your comfort zone.

As we move beyond our fears it is natural to feel a sense of elation. It is appropriate to give thanks for our release from the captivity of our fears. At the same time our spirits are vulnerable at these times to excessive pride in the illusion of our personal strength. When we do not immediately move away from such illusionary thinking we place ourselves in extreme emotional and spiritual jeopardy.

Enter into a study of spiritual warfare (see *Ephesians 6:10-20*). Study the elements of Satan's temptation of Jesus in the wilderness (*Matthew 4:1-11*). We will look further on the presence of evil in Encounter 13.

Participate in a vision quest led by a qualified and trained leader.

As Jesus called people to follow him they began living in a new reality. As they developed a new identity the disciples of Jesus sometimes changed even their names. Open yourself to receiving a new name (*Revelation 2:17*).

Schools and retreat centers are emerging throughout the country that teach wilderness survival skills.

Skilled trackers can now be found in most areas of the country. Consider training in bird and animal tracking and behavior to develop hypersensitive awareness to your surroundings in any environment or situation.

Backpack into the wilderness each season of the year.

Develop a diet that best suits the warrior aspect of your life.

Examine warrior traditions from various cultures past and present. Consider Native American, Japanese, African, and other traditions.

Find a warrior-focused mentor from whom you can receive counsel regarding your direction in this area. Find a person to whom you can confess your failings, especially your fears.

The Warrior in the Wilderness

Within indigenous hunter gatherer cultures throughout the world, there typically exists a warrior class that is responsible for the physical protection of the community and especially for the hunting aspect of its food gathering.

As protector, the warrior must be physically strong and continually alert for danger. As hunter, the warrior must be intimately aquatinted with the surrounding environment.

In hunter gather societies, the warrior is almost always a male member of the community. We believe that the elemental skills that connect the warrior to the natural world are now necessary for both women and men to employ for the sake of reconnecting to creation, to ourselves, to others and to the lifeforce.

When the warrior enters the forest, she must not call attention to herself, she must learn to blend into the environment with keenly developed senses. The community's survival is dependent on the warrior's skill, nothing can be done carelessly; a single careless step can undo a day's hunt.

The warrior is attuned to the movement of birds and animals, the position of the sun, the direction of the wind. Tracking becomes a form of reading the story of the day's events upon the forest floor.

The indigenous warrior is present with the life she encounters in the wilderness, she does not see herself superior to that life so much as she sees herself intimately a part of it. Birds and animals are regarded with great respect, the different aspects of their being teach the warrior about her own life.

Throughout childhood, the warrior is trained through the informal mentoring of skilled adult warriors. Skills are developed not just for the sake of the child's future and wellbeing but with a consciousness of the future wellbeing of entire community. Growing strong in body, mind, and spirit is seen as both an individual and communal achievement.

History is interpreted through the eyes of the culture recording it. Historical judgments are made according to the way of life that has been deemed right, successful, advancing, and civilized over and against what is deemed unsuccessful, wrong, backward, and uncivilized.

Since the Renaissance, western civilization has bought into a paradigm of continual advancement; believing that humanity can create a better world through scientific and technological advancement. Much benefit has come to humanity through this world view, and so has great damage at great cost to our spiritual and physical wellbeing.

European Christians came to North America believing in their divinely sanctioned right; their "Manifest Destiny" to conquer the land and its peoples for their own ends and the good of civilization.

Darwinism and its theories related to the natural selection of the fittest further bolstered the assurance of the superiority of the civilized. The consequence of such views allowed the "civilized" to view the "uncivilized" as subhuman and excused horrific treatment.

The ensuing extermination of peoples so deeply connected to the natural world has now come back to haunt us. We are only beginning to see what we have lost through their destruction. We are beginning to understand that so much of what they had we now desperately need.

We need not only seek forgiveness for our own blindness, we need to help reclaim the foundational values of these almost lost cultures as we open ourselves to learn from them.

The Warrior Prayer

Holy Creator
Father of all tribes,
Mother source of all life,
Guide me into the heartbeat
Of your created order,
That your life in me
Would be a guide to others.

Teach me to see You
In every living thing,
In my physical body
And the body of the Earth,
In sister and brother,
In companion and stranger,
In friend and enemy.

Teach me Great Spirit
To walk straight like the fox,
To dive into dark waters like the gannet,
To leap free like the dolphin.

Open me to the wisdom of the raven,
To the joy of the otter,
To the industry of the beaver,
To the agile quickness of the deer,
To the fierce flight of the peregrine.

Holy, all powerful lifeforce
Send me forth as your warrior
Into the battle unafraid,
To return evil with good,
Hatred with love,
Forever knowing that my enemies
Are not my fellow human beings,
But principalities that choke off life
And powers that pervert life.

Forgive me my arrogance,
Trusting in the illusion
Of my own strength.
Help me in my weakness
To reject violence in all its forms;
Violence in thought, word or deed.

Holy Presence ,
Equip me for battle
With your Holy armor;
The belt of truth,
The shield of faith to quench the flaming arrows
Of the evil one,
The helmet of salvation,
The sword of the Spirit
Which is the Word,
Wearing marching boots to proclaim
The gospel of peace.
Help me to disregard winning
As the world interprets winning,
To seize the victory
Already won in Christ,
To stand firm in the battle for justice,
To protect the weak,
To stand with the oppressed.

Holy Spirit
In your purifying fire
Burn away all impurity,
Lead me away from the thousand deaths
That rob me of life.
Lead me unto the death.
That leads me to life.

Bathe my simple dwelling,
In the light of your presence.
Help me to choose wisely
From the abundance you provide;
Food that nourishes muscle,
Bone, blood, marrow, every cell,
And strengthens me for the mission
That brings glory only to you.

All continues by your will,
By your command the sun rises,
By your decree the sun will set.

In death
My soul sails over the lake of fire
Into the new country.
Where my ancestors wait
Within the eternal dwelling;
Mother and Father,
Sisters and brothers,
Friends and enemies,
My home as ever
In you.

Applying the Encounter to Our Lives

- In light of this encounter's understanding of warrior, think of women who have lived within the last hundred years who fit this definition of warrior. What men come to mind?

- Consider examples from the New Testament Gospels in which Jesus is a warrior.

- Consider the difference between the world's view of warrior and the warrior described within this encounter.

- What does it require to be a warrior?

- What aspects of warrior would you personally consider working on?

- Is there an area of social justice that you feel led to consider giving time to?

- If you are using this guide within a group, is there an area of social justice that you are being led to as a group?

- What circumstance might arise in your everyday life that would call upon you to be a warrior?

Meditation Exercise

Set your timer to 10 minutes. The warrior identity is one of strength and confidence. The warrior's concern is for the wellbeing and protection of the weak and oppressed. The warrior's foundational trust is in a power greater than herself.

Consider a walking meditation. Walk with intentionality, your back arched, shoulders back, head erect and looking forward. Walk in the woods, a park or down a busy street in a city. Put aside fear and self-consciousness. Tune in to your surroundings, sights, sounds, everything around you.

For the next 10 minutes, walk in the spirit of the warrior.

Repeat this exercise daily until the next encounter.

Mystic

The mystic is one who sees beneath the surface, who sees the lifeforce in every aspect of creation.

The focus of the mystic is on an intimate union with the lifeforce. As human beings we innately long for this connection that brings us into relationship with one another and all creation. The mystic is not afraid of desire. The mystic understands that all desire has at its core the desire to perfectly unite with the lifeforce.

A great empty void exists within our souls when this union is neither identified nor nurtured.

A Mystic within the new reality introduced by Jesus is:

- One who sees deeply, beyond the surface.
- One who sees beneath.
- One who sees within.
- One who focuses on the development of the soul through an intimate relationship to, and a union with the lifeforce.
- One attuned to the presence of the lifeforce within creation.
- One attuned to the multidimensionality of creation.
- One aware of the Holy Spirit's power, presence, availability.
- One who accesses gifts of the Holy Spirit.
- One who prays in the Spirit.

- One who seeks power beyond self, beyond words, programs.

- One who takes time in the "desert," in the wilderness, the empty and barren places away from the frenzied pace, where renewal and direction can take place.

- One comfortable with silence.

- One who loves scripture.

- One who respects the holiness of the lifeforce.

- One who takes hold of the life that is really life.

Mystic Exercises

Pray daily for a deeper connection to every aspect of creation. Begin each day with a prayer of thanksgiving.

Spend time outdoors each day. Establish a "sit spot" no more than five minutes from your home. The site you choose could be within a cluster of trees, a park (especially if you live in the city), or your backyard. Be aware of the sounds you hear, the movement of birds and animals, the sky, the wind, the temperature, the position of the sun.

Begin by spending five or ten minutes at the site and increase to fifteen or twenty minutes over time. Observe the differences in each day, changes as the seasons come and go. You are learning to be attentive.

Seek to use everything you encounter to draw you closer to the lifeforce, yourself, and to all creation. Keep a daily journal recording the presence of the lifeforce through the day. Write out prayers. Let your personal voice come through, your deepest thoughts, your sorrows and joys.

How has Christ revealed himself to you in this day? How has Christ spoken to you? Who has Christ sent you? Are you living in joy?

Within each day, create a space for silence. Remove yourself as much as possible from all outside stimulation. Move toward a condition and attitude of solitude. Learn to quiet yourself, become aware of your breath, fill your lungs with a slow deliberate deep breath, and exhale slowly, expelling all the air out of your lungs. Take in the fresh life-giving air, push out the used air that can no longer serve your body.

Consider taking a yoga class to increase your flexibility, strengthen muscles, to practice controlled breathing, for balance and coordination, and for relaxation.

The mystic is a poet. Keep a poetry journal. The Psalms come to us from the poet, expressing the presence of the lifeforce within creation, within the best of times and the worst of times. Live in a spirit of attentiveness. Record through your poetry what you see, feel, touch, smell, think, sense. Have you been afraid or anxious? Have you experienced desire, brokenness, loneliness, sorrow, laughter, hope, joy?

The mystic is an artist. Drawing is a foundational activity for the artist. Keep a drawing journal. Draw from life, draw at your "sit spot," draw trees, clouds, people, animals. Drawing forces a deeper seeing. Drawing can be a form of meditation.

Consider taking a drawing or painting class. Visit art galleries and museums to observe the work of other artists.

Let music be an integral part of your life. Examine how different forms of music speak to you and nurture your spirit.

Experiment with different forms of dance and different forms of music.

- Learn to play a musical instrument
- Put your poetry to song.
- Sing.
- Sing songs of praise.
- Sing songs of longing.
- Sing songs of thanksgiving.
- Sing songs of healing.
- Sing songs of loss.
- Sing songs of joy.

The mystic is in love with life. The mystic lives in joyful abandon. Praise the lifeforce that you are alive in this day.

The mystic is one who sees beneath the surface. This acute perception can create a vulnerable spirit. The mystic guards her spirit from depression and anxiety. Sharing with another person who is spiritually mature on at least a monthly basis is critical to the mystic's well-being. For one who is more naturally a mystic the intentional development of her warrior and monk personalities becomes critically important to spiritual and emotional well-being.

Consider very seriously finding a spiritual director.

Study the mystical connections that indigenous cultures have with creation. Examine the culture's rituals and arts.

Consider visiting a monastery that opens its doors for spiritual retreats and offers spiritual direction.

Explore the development of Christianity in Ireland. Explore Celtic Christianity.

Consider a pilgrimage to the island of Iona in Scotland, the Taizé community in France, and the ancient Neolithic and early Christian sites in Ireland.

The meal is a sacred time. Eating carelessly breaks our connectedness to the web of life. Develop a respect for food and a consciousness of where the food on your plate comes from.

The mystic is an artist. The artist is not afraid of exposing and engaging her wounds.

The Mystic in the Desert

A migration of Christians into the deserts of Egypt, Palestine, Arabia, and Persia began in the fourth century. These people would be known as the desert fathers and mothers and would be regarded as the first Christian hermits.

By the fourth century Christianity's enormous popularity and growth began to take a toll on its original vision. It was departing from its radical communal beginnings as an alternative to the worldly quests for wealth, power, and prestige as it became the official religion of the Roman empire.

Those who were fleeing to the desert were both repudiating what Christianity was becoming and seeking the salvation of body, mind, and spirit that Christ had offered.

The desert fathers and mothers believed that they were fleeing a disaster. They believed that life as it was meant to be lived, life within the new reign of the lifeforce introduced by Christ was in the process of being replaced by religious practices.

They could no longer tolerate passively drifting along accepting the values, mindset and direction of a society that they saw on a collision course with the new reign Christ had inaugurated.

On the surface, Christianity appeared to have reached a zenith of success. The emperor was now a Christian. The sign of the cross was becoming the sign of the state. Laws were being established against paganism, it's writings and practices.

For those who were taking flight into the desert, Christianity's absorption into the culture spelled disaster for their souls. They were not disengaging from life so much as they were seeking to more deeply engage in it.

The desert provided a purifying cauldron. In the desert a battle waited to be fought for heart and mind. The desert did not free them from personal struggle, it provided an atmosphere of raw clarity within the struggle. In the vast sparseness of the desert, it was difficult, even absurd to fake living. In the desert the distractions that numbed the mind, the spirit, and soul evaporated. All that separates from the fullness the lifeforce intends lay clearly exposed, that which leads to life begins to be illuminated.

The desert fathers and mothers had walked into the wilderness in much the same way Jesus had; forced by the enemy of their souls to deal with all that would pull them away from full devotion to the lifeforce.

The desert mothers and fathers sought their truest selves in Christ and in doing so did battle with their false selves. Their writings are gifts of wisdom that reveal the rich fruit gained by their full engagement with illusion and reality.

They lived in caves and the simplest of huts. They sought to give every moment of the day to the Holy Presence. In the wilderness they recognized their smallness, they were humbled as they reconnected to their place within the magnificence of creation; their senses expanded.

Their wisdom preserved in their writings; is a gift to our age, as is their simplicity of spirit, their clarity, their devotion, their poverty and their power. The fullness of their lives beckons us.

The desert today is both a physical place to which we are called to enter to regain our lives and a spiritual condition, a state of being that we carry into the world. When we step into the desert we step away from illusion into a raw engagement with life that is both frightening and liberating.

We step into the desert to engage the powers and principalities that seek to dominate our lives, to engage the demons, fears, addictions and dependencies that have so robbed us of life.

We step into the desert to embrace solitude, stillness, silence; to quiet our spirits, to engage the natural order of creation; listening, trusting. We step into knowing and not knowing, into mystery, into fullness of being.

MYSTIC PRAYER

Holy lifeforce,
Holy Jesus,
Holy Spirit,
One revealed in three,
Present in every living thing
In every moment,

Holy mystery
Beyond defining,
Open me to the mystery,
To see beneath the surface,
To live within your depths.

Come to me beloved,
Embrace me
In the beauty of your completeness.

In the midst of storm,
Through thunder, lightning, and violent wind,
Help me to live in stillness.

As the world races
And humanity falls exhausted,
Quiet my spirit,
Lift me to dancing.

Open me to my smallness

Within a galaxy of 200 billion suns,
Within a universe of millions of galaxies,
Make me smaller still;
The tiniest speck
But in your mercy
A speck of light.

Holy Spirit walk with me
As you walked with Christ
Into the desert,
The vast and empty space.
Walk me through the Valley
Of the shadow of death.
Expose my clinging
To the half-life,
To fear.
Help me to awaken
From empty dreaming
So that I may become
One with you
And all creation.

Comfort me in my loneliness
So that I may comfort the lonely.

Through my suffering
Lead me to those who suffer.
Anoint my weeping
that I might weep with the brokenhearted.
Use even my darkness
To bring forth light.
In my healing
Anoint me to heal.

Fill me with such abandon
That laughter becomes my second language.

Holy Presence,
Baptize me in your Holy Spirit
To speak in both human and angelic tongues.

Holy Spirit
Consume me in your holy fire.

Nurture the artist within me.
May the work of my hands,
Impart the essence of my soul.

Allow me to enter into:
The song of the hermit thrush on the lower branches,
The beating heart of the winter wren on the stone wall,
The flight of the kittiwake off the cliffs ledge above the waves,
The eyes of the barred owl in the winter night.

Send me to those who need to be seen.
Remove the stone from the entrance
To the cave that shelters my heart,
To see as you see,
To love as you love,

To embody in my life
The message of the gospel
Revealed and set free in Christ.

After drawing my last breath
My body will merge into the earth
To be taken by spring rains
Into the streams flowing into rivers
To the oceans that touch every shore,
As my soul
Flows into You.

Applying the Encounter to Our Lives

- In light of this understanding of mystic think of women and men who have lived within the last hundred years who fit this definition of mystic

- Consider examples from the New Testament Gospels in which Jesus is a mystic.

- In what area of the arts do you most closely identify; music, literature, poetry, painting, film-making, sewing, drama, other?

- Is there an area of the arts in which you would like to grow more involved?

- Do you feel a close connection to nature? How might this connection be more deeply nurtured?

- Are you conscious of the Holy Spirit's presence in your life? How is the presence of the Holy Spirit manifested in your life?

- How might you nurture a deeper connection to the lifeforce?

- Do you pray in tongues?

- What are your Spiritual Gifts?

- Are there one or two of the mystic exercises found within this that you were drawn to?

Meditation Exercise

Set your timer to 11 minutes.

Find a place outside in which you can comfortably sit. Ideally this will be a short walk from home, in a nearby woods or field, a park or just outside your front door.

Allow all your senses to experience the place you have chosen. What are the sounds you hear? Is there human generated noise? Are there bird, animal or insect sounds? What do you see? What do you smell? Is there a breeze? What is the temperature?

What is the feel of this place?

What lies beneath you? Travel in your mind and imagination deeper and deeper into the Earth.

Travel in your mind and imagination into the sky above. Go as far as you can imagine. What lies above you?

Experience in your Spirit your place within everything that is.

Repeat this exercise daily until the next encounter.

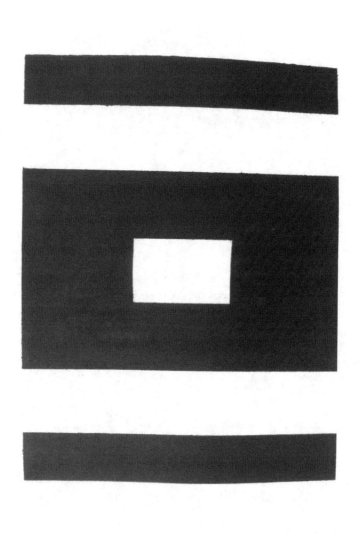

Monk

The monk is a woman or man, married or single, who lives a life of ordered devotion to the lifeforce within community; focusing on service, teaching, simplicity, spiritual direction and hospitality.

Our lives are incomplete apart from a covenanted relationship with sisters and brothers seeking to walk in "the Way" of Jesus.

Living simply, peacefully, together; modeling another way of living within the new reign of the lifeforce introduced by Jesus, is the daily focus of the monk. A monk living within the community of Jesus is:

- One who is devoted to the lifeforce through an ordered life.
- One within a community of others.
- One who is available to others through service and hospitality.
- One who subjects to authority of the lifeforce and community.
- One who can be alone and with others.
- One who is able and willing to serve in a priestly role.
- One who prays, meditates.
- One who has let go of an idealized image of self.
- One who expresses love for the lifeforce through love for others.
- One who recognizes her incompleteness without a community of brothers and sisters.
- One in whose life the fruit of the Holy Spirit is present.
- One who sees scripture as the guidebook to daily life.
- One who seeks daily to die to self and to live in Christ.

Monk Exercises

Incorporate the rhythm of the monastic "hours" into the routine of your daily life. As you awaken in the morning give praise for the new day before you (Vigils/Matins). Offer a prayer of thanksgiving as the sun rises (Lauds). Just prior to beginning the work of the day seek the guidance and blessing of the lifeforce (Prime). During a mid-morning break, stop for a moment remembering the presence of the lifeforce, perhaps combining the remembrance with the ritual of coffee or tea (Terse). At noontime break (Sext) over lunch read or memorize a table grace. During mid-afternoon break (None) pray for a local, national and world concern. Prior to supper (Vespers) read a small section of scripture. As you prepare to go to bed, offer a prayer of gratitude for Christ's presence with you through the day (Compline).

The monk lives within a community of faith. As our lives deepen and we begin to live more intentionally within the rhythm of God's created order, our understanding of the importance of community to the life we are seeking increases.

- Our community worships together,
- Our community shares meals together,
- Our community prays together,
- Our community seeks to live together in wholeness,
- We forgive one another, we love one another.

Consider how you can deepen your relationship with brothers and sisters. Begin by calling together others who want to be more supportive and accountable to one another. Explore ways to break from the frantic pace of our societies consumer driven obsession. Seek to live more simply. Discover the joy of simplicity. Monks live in simple cells with few material possessions to distract them. Create a sense of order within your living space. Begin by cleaning out closets and storage spaces. Get rid of anything you have not worn or used for a year. Over time, go through each room of the house.

All monks take on the servant role within the community. What act of service can you provide within the community? What act of service can you carry into the world? Focus especially on caring for the "least", on caring for those who are not seen as being of value or not seen at all.

Spend at least a few hours each week laboring with your hands.

The monk is a gardener. If you don't have a garden consider starting one. Begin very small. Growing your own food helps to connect you to your food and to the provision of the lifeforce.

The monk's participation in the arts is often from a utilitarian perspective. Consider learning how to make pots on a pottery wheel. Make a set of cups and dishes. Take up weaving or woodworking.

Participate in a weekly communion service. Consider experimenting for a period of time with a daily Eucharist.

The priesthood of all believers was a cornerstone of the early church. What is your priestly role within community? How can you be a priest to your brothers and sisters?

Find time for solitude within your community life.

What might it mean to live a sacramental life? What elements might be included in a sacramental life?

Experiment with community dance. Incorporate dance within worship.

Incorporate the spiritual disciplines of prayer, fasting, study, meditation, service, simplicity, solitude, confession and worship into your daily routine.

Meet with a spiritual director on a regular basis.

The Monk in the Garden

The monk aspect of our being calls us to look to the spiritual and physical needs of the community. The monk's role in the garden bridges both. Through the garden we experience the connection between the lifeforce's provision and our cultivation. The physical fruits of the garden sustain our physical bodies. The fruits of connection to the lifeforce's created order nurtures our spiritual communal body.

The garden is a place of deep significance throughout the Bible. Upon creating Man and Woman, the lifeforce places them in a garden. Within the Garden of Eden, woman and man live in perfect harmony with all creation. They know neither fear nor shame. Their physical needs are met through the provision of the garden.

Man and woman come to a point of rebellion against the lifeforce, their harmonious relationship to creation ends, they experience fear and shame and they are exiled from the garden.

Jesus Christ is sent by the lifeforce to restore us to the relationship we knew in the garden. In this sense, Jesus becomes the new Adam (*Romans 5:10-12*).

As his suffering and impending death approach, Jesus goes to a garden to pray that there might be another way. In the garden, Jesus receives into his spirit his understanding of the lifeforce's will and purpose. Through this act of acceptance, Jesus reverses the consequences of Adam and Eve's separation from creation. The opportunity of living again within the harmonious relationship we knew in the original garden is made possible.

As Jesus finishes praying the temple soldiers storm into the garden to arrest Jesus. He is taken prisoner; removed from the garden, interrogated through the night, put on mock trial, condemned, tortured and crucified.

Jesus dies on the cross, is taken down and buried in a garden. The tomb of death within the garden becomes the womb of eternal life. In the garden Jesus comes alive.

The first person to see Jesus in His resurrected state is Mary Magdalene. She comes to the garden in the early morning to visit the tomb. She "mistakes" Jesus for the gardener. He speaks her name, "Mary", and she knows him.

Jesus is the gardener of the emerging new realm. The seed of His body buried in the garden springs to life, producing fruit that will seed a new generation of the lifeforce's children (*Romans 8:14-16*). This new generation of sons and daughters will accept the lifeforce's original charge in Genesis to care for, respect and live within the harmonious heartbeat of the created order of the lifeforce.

The garden is a place where cultivation and care produce life sustaining fruit. As we live within a lifeforce consciousness our understanding of the full significance of the garden expands.

Maintaining some form of physical garden, even if it is very small, places us actively within the rhythm of creation. As gardener monks we connect our physical feeding to our spiritual feeding.

MONK PRAYER

Holy of Holies
Father of order, mother embracing,
Son leading,
Spirit empowering;

Give us this day
The bread of the earth for our bodies,
The bread of your body for our Earth.

Help us to enter the hours
In reverent worship,
The day in constant prayer

We pray your blessing on our communion,
Upon the bread,
Your body broken for us,
Upon the wine,
Your blood shed for us.

As these elements enter our physical bodies
Dispersing to organs, cells, muscle and bone,
So let your presence
Disperse to touch each aspect of our
Individual spiritual bodies
And our body life within community.

Bless the work of our hands
Open us to the giftedness of our work.
May our work be a blessing to the community
In service to Christ Jesus.

Your blessing Holy Creator
Upon our gardens
Through every season;
In spring planting
In summer tending
In fall harvest
In winter rest

We give thanks for the bounty of the garden,
For all food that nourishes our bodies;
For carrots and tomatoes,
Potatoes and lettuce,
Cucumbers, beans, broccoli, cauliflower
Beets and onions;

For strawberries and raspberries,
Apples and pears,
Grapes and plums.

We give thanks for the bounty of the garden,
For all flowers that nourish our souls;
For daffodils and tulips,
For mourning glories and sunflowers,
For zinnias, petunias, geraniums,
Delphinium and daisies.

We pray that the fruit of the Holy spirit
Would be nurtured in the garden of our souls,
Love
Joy
Peace
Patience

Kindness
Goodness
Gentleness
Faithfulness
Self-control

Awaken us to the giftedness
Of the seasons of the year
And each season of our lives.

We thank you Holy Spirit
For the planting of spiritual gifts
Within our brothers and sisters;
Bless and nurture;
The utterance of wisdom
Apostles
The utterance of knowledge
Prophets
Faith
Teachers
Gifts of healing
Deeds of power
Working of miracles
Prophecy
Forms of assistance
Discernment of spirits
Forms of leadership
Various tongues
Various kinds of tongues
Interpretations of tongues

Jesus
Emmanuel, Holy Presence with us,
Keep us mindful that you are within all
Who come to our door.
We pray for the gift of hospitality.
We pray for a loving spirit,

For a teaching spirit.
May our life together be our primary teaching.

Help me to strive to be least among
My sisters and brothers,
To kneel at their feet with basin and towel,
As Christ washed the disciples feet,
And called us to do likewise.

Bless our humble cells,
Our dwelling places
For solitary retreat
For rest
For study
For prayer
For sleep.

As sister death comes to me
And I leave the earthly table,
My body returned to the clay
From which I was formed,
You, O ever living Christ
Welcome the essential
Eternal part of me
To your eternal table.

Applying the Encounter to Our Lives

- In light of this understanding of monk, think of women and men who have lived within the last hundred years who fit the definition of Monk.

- Consider examples from the New Testament Gospels in which Jesus is a monk.

- What aspects of a monk's life appeal to you?

- What aspects of a monk's life do not appeal to you?

- Where do you find community?

- How do you feel about your prayer life? Your study life?

- In what ways do you serve within your community?

- In what ways do you provide hospitality to others?

- Are there specific aspects of the monk's life that you would like to nurture to a greater degree in your own life?

- Is there an intentional order within your day

Meditation Exercises

Set your timer to 12 minutes

The Fruit of the Holy Spirit listed in the New Testament book of *Galatians 5:22-23* is composed of nine states of being:

- **Love**
- **Peace**
- **Kindness**
- **Gentleness**
- **Self-Control**
- **Joy**
- **Patience**
- **Goodness**
- **Faithfulness**

Make a list of these nine words. You are encouraged to memorize the list.

For this meditation slowly chant each word. Chant these words in sequence for perhaps two minutes, spending approximately one minute on each sequence. Through the next twelve minutes chant each word for approximately one minute on each word (The single word could be repeated four or five times within the minute).

Allow your spirit to embrace each word.

Consider making this chant a daily ritual.

Repeat this exercise daily until the next encounter.

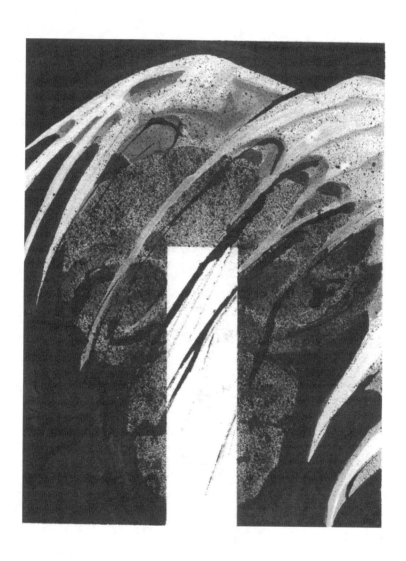

The Presence of Evil

We live within a culture that has little understanding or respect for the power of evil over its individual and corporate life. Evil is identified with "the other," other people, other nations. A daily battle rages for control of our hearts and minds. Our vulnerability to fear, confusion, depression, anger, addiction, and emptiness is directly related to our inability to recognize the power and presence of evil.

> *"For our struggle is not against flesh and blood, but against principalities, against the powers of this present darkness, against the spiritual forces of evil in heavenly places."* Ephesians 6:12, NASB.

Strongholds

It is a mistake to think that our struggle is against people. Our struggle against evil is a battle against subversive spirits, forces of deception, strongholds of power.

There are destructive spirits within every family, demons that continually threaten the wellbeing, peace and harmony of the family unit and each individual within it.

There are destructive powers operating over whole groups of people, over regions, over nations, over political, religious and corporate entities.

Principalities and powers hold tremendous sway over our lives. Resistance to the evil produced by these powers must be based upon a foundation of love, of justice and peace. Violence and hatred, even within what appear to be just causes empowers evil.

Jesus is the model in the confrontation of the powers and principalities that continually seek to dominate the lives of the most vulnerable. Jesus was continually doing battle with demons that subvert individual lives and principalities that enslave societies. In the short period of his ministry it might have appeared that his mission had failed, that his confrontation of evil had been lost. Time has proved otherwise.

Awaken

Spiritual awakening opens our eyes to the presence of the lifeforce all around us, within us and within every created thing. When our spiritual eyes are opened we see that everything is connected. This new vision has a dark side. Our eyes are also opened to the presence of evil around us and the power evil wields throughout the world.

The beauty of the web of connection within every created thing is tainted by the power of evil to threaten and decay that beauty. The foundational understanding of these encounters are based upon the idea that a spiritual awakening has become critical to human survival. Humanity is blindly racing toward what it has called global advancement without examining the future costs of this advancement. It is as if the train has left the station and increasing its speed to the point it cannot be stopped without catastrophe.

It is easy to think about evil only as bad things being done by bad people. More often it is about good things becoming over time perverted.

We have been taught to trust that things go up and down in life and that eventually humans figure out their problems and correct them. To some extent it is true that human adaptability is part of human evolution. But as the world grows smaller through technology, globalization and immigration, and larger through massive population growth, the world's problems grow exponentially larger at an ever increasing rate of speed.

In contemporary western society, a corporate fear has emerged that is rarely talked about. There is a foreboding sense that things are not going to get better. There exists a growing corporate consciousness that something terrible is about to happen, has begun already to happen, that things around us are falling apart at an alarming rate of speed. The depth of our corporate fear continually escalates as political, religious, educational, financial and environmental systems continue to deteriorate around us.

The ever increasing apocalyptic themes in contemporary films and literature speak to the dis-ease of the culture. Addiction in some form now touches every person's life. We spend a great deal of energy, time and money suppressing the reality of an evil dominion that has largely taken control of our lives.

We live in an age of addiction and addictions are primarily about numbing the anxiety that dominions of evil create within us. We know that something is very wrong around us that is now reaching within us.

Awakening spiritually opens us to the life that is truly life. Awakening spiritually opens us to the barriers in realizing that life. Awakening demands that we admit to the addictions we have succumbed to in order to numb our fears; addictions that have become an integral part of our personal and corporate lives.

Awakened individuals need awakened communities if they are going to grow into the depths that Jesus realized and hoped for his followers. The new community of Jesus is dependent upon each member identifying their own demons. Each member needs the understanding, prayer, forgiveness, love, support and challenge of the community. We dare not be in this battle alone.

Addiction

With a desperate need to numb ourselves the choices available to us are legion. Drugs and alcohol are the most obvious. Many of our choices seem at least at first harmless. Then one day we realize we can no longer feel safe without being hooked up to technology, the cell phone must be in our hand, the computer has to be checked and checked again, the T.V. must remain on even when we leave the room. We can no longer sit in silence alone, we have an addiction. One day we realize we are no longer eating because we are hungry, we are eating to fill another kind of emptiness.

Escaping into thoughts about sex is a way of numbing our reality and temporarily suppressing our anxiety. Pornography is now just a computer click away. Entertainment is increasingly sexualized and more violent. Watching graphic violence is for some the drug of choice. With each new season of television the torturous murders must become increasingly violent to equal last year's sensations.

The accumulation of wealth has become an obsession and more is never enough. For those without wealth gambling becomes a way to seek it. The state not only supports gambling it now provides it.

The list of obsessions goes on and on. For some, watching and listening to particular slants on the news becomes an everyday, all day affair. Conservative and liberal are no longer simply political stances, they have for many become all-consuming ideologies. For some, religion becomes an obsession. In each of these cases one's understandings are seen as superior to the beliefs of others to the point that the other becomes the enemy.

The technological modern world is one of isolation. How do we battle the loneliness, the emptiness and gnawing anxiety? Drugs do work, at least for a time they numb us. Then the unsettled feeling arises again. A little larger dose is needed, and later a little larger.

We go shopping, not necessarily because there is something we need, but looking for something we want. Buying induces a temporary high that masks the emptiness.

Are these drugs, these obsessions, evil? Generally not, but they numb us to evils emergence. It begins with small moral lapses, lies, inconsequential cheating, compromises; until slowly the moral compass disappears and the lies get bigger and more and more becomes lost.

Spiritual awakening opens us to the potential of liberation that can be found within our connection to the lifeforce. Our connection to the lifeforce opens us to the daily battle against forces of suppression, domination and fear; to dominions of power entrenched in high places.

The talons of the powers and principalities have been driven deep into the skin of our culture. The pain of this piercing is clear even as the source of the anguish goes unrecognized.

Evil's Rising

While evil is always present in the world, there are periods throughout history in which its dominion rises. Ethnic cleansings and genocides occur in the ancient writings of the Old Testament and have continued to the present day. Religions; all religions, have committed atrocities that continue to this present day. The near enslavement of women, the abuse and oppression that women have experienced throughout history continues to this present day.

The horrendous treatment, that those whose sexual orientation has been deemed unacceptable, continues to this present day.

We are only beginning to understand the depth of the savagery of slavery within the history of the United States. The blindness to this prolonged domination of evil is unimaginable. This period of evil continues in many forms to this present day.

The rise of Nazi Germany in the last century is an example of a whole region of the world succumbing to evil. The accepted mass extermination of Jews transported humanity to incredible levels of inhumanity.

The dropping of nuclear bombs on Hiroshima and Nagasaki to end an evil war ushered in a new period of evil.

All of this savagery has been part of the human condition since the beginning of human existence. All of the technological advances and scientific discoveries of modern times have not erased war, poverty, slavery, oppression, racism and greed. Evil continues to stalk humanity.

A New Path, A New Humanity

Humanity, for the sake of its continued existence cannot continue on this same path. On some level all of us know this. We know things cannot keep going the way they always have. And herein lies the purpose of these encounters. Humanity needs to reinvent itself. The technological age we live in may not give us time to evolve. We find ourselves, as a species, in need of a radical spiritual awakening that will catch us up to the technological world we have created. We must, in some form, become a new species or sub species. We must be transformed from homo sapiens to homo spiritus.

Two thousand years ago Jesus was trying to tell us that things cannot keep going like this. We must be reborn. He gave himself to this rebirth prior to his public ministry. He walked into the desert and for forty days battled against the forces of evil that sought to dominate his life. He was tempted to continue being run by forces that have dominated humanity; to be in control, to be spectacular, to be special.

In resisting the domination of principalities and powers in his life, Jesus became the first of a new species of human beings.

The time has come for each of us to walk into the desert, to step apart for a time, to walk away from addictions and obsessions that numb our senses. In the desert we confront our fears and vain, destructive strivings. We open ourselves to the lifeforce and a power beyond ourselves. We face the principalities and powers that we have allowed to play us. We give ourselves to a power greater than they are. We give ourselves to rebirth and to the new way of being alive that Jesus began.

Applying the Encounter to Our Lives

- "Our battle is not against flesh and blood." What does this mean? Can you give examples of how this is true?

- Give examples of existing principalities and powers.

- Has your life been affected by evil? Are you willing to share your experience?

- How is spiritual awakening important related to the presence of evil?

- Do you have an addiction/obsession that in some way temporarily eases your anxiety?

- Do you believe that there is a power greater than the power of evil?

- Is it possible for humanity to change, for a new way of living to be adopted by humanity? Will this happen?

- Can you change?

- In light of the continuous plague of evil throughout history what is your hope for the future?

- If you are going through this guide with a group, how can the group help you?

- Consider taking some time away from the daily routine of your life. Consider entering into the desert, to spending a period of time without distractions facing the negative forces that can dominate too much of your life.

Meditation Exercise

We have just completed a lesson on the presence of evil in the world. While it is a difficult subject to face, it is a dangerous subject to ignore. How can we recognize evil and do battle against it without our spirits being overcome with grief, sadness, depression or fear?

Spiritual awakening opens us to both the presence of the lifeforce and the presence of evil. Within our awakening we experience rebirth; we become in our spirits children of the lifeforce.

No matter what we must face in this life we trust the lifeforce to hold us in each moment and forever. This does not mean we will always maintain a feeling of peace and wellbeing, but even within anxiety and fear we trust that we are being held. We are held by a force greater than evil.

Set your timer to 13 minutes. Thirteen minutes will be a long time for this exercise. You might try setting your timer for two minutes and through the next six days add two minutes each day.

Begin this meditation by repeating the phrase, "Greater is the power of the lifeforce than the power of evil." After repeating this phrase several times, enter into peace. Do not think about peace, be at peace. Move in your spirit from peace to joy. Your joy is born from your peace. Breathe in peace, breathe out joy. Even if you hold this sense of joy for only seconds this is a beginning. From joy move to laughter.

Repeat this exercise daily until the next encounter.

The Spirit

All of the gospels; Matthew, Mark, Luke, and John record the baptism of Jesus prior to the beginning of his public ministry. As Jesus emerged from the water the Holy Spirit hovered over him.

At the beginning of creation the Spirit had hovered over the waters from which all life would emerge. At the beginning of a new creation of humanity the Spirit again hovered over the water as Jesus was baptized. This was the beginning of a new baptism, a new emergence of life, a baptism of Spirit that would be poured out upon all who would enter the life that Jesus was demonstrating. Jesus is the firstborn of a new creation, the first to receive a new flowing of the Holy Spirit.

Immediately following his baptism, Jesus goes into the desert wilderness. He does not go alone; he is accompanied by the Holy Spirit. Jesus had been both baptized in water and baptized in the Spirit. Jesus is accompanied, guided and empowered by the Spirit.

Jesus does battle with evil in the desert; he is tempted by the agenda of principalities and powers. He is pulled by that agenda. Jesus is not just going through the motions of temptation; he desires all that is offered. He is pulled as we are pulled.

What the powers offer is not evil in itself, what the powers offer is the path to emptiness that spawns evil. Jesus desires worldly power, he wants to be relevant and spectacular, he wants to be seen as favored by God.

Through the sight given him by the Spirit, Jesus is able to see where the path of the powers leads; to recognition, position, wealth, comfort, power. Why would he say no? Why would Jesus instead step onto a path that would lead to rejection, poverty, humiliation, torture, crucifixion and death?

Jesus could see through the eyes of the Spirit that no matter how wealthy, recognized, powerful, comfortable, he could become, that life would end and be done. The life that Jesus rejected was not a bad life; it was a sad and ultimately pointless life.

Jesus chose the life he did, not only to save humanity, Jesus was human, he chose the life that would also save him.

There is a crucifixion awaiting us all, a picking up of our own cross, a path that leads to the death of the old self as we walk away from the call of the principalities and powers. We forfeit our lives to save them. The control that we so long sought to maintain now feels like shackles.

Following his resurrection Jesus told his followers; about a hundred and twenty women and men, to go to Jerusalem, meet together in an upper room and wait for the empowerment of the Spirit to come upon them. Before their new life could begin, they would need to be born anew, they would need to receive the indwelling of the Spirit.

Following the death and resurrection of Jesus a new community of faith begins to dramatically emerge. The central factor within this extraordinary emergence is the outpouring of the Spirit upon the community.

Previously, throughout the Old Testament, the Spirit is bestowed upon individuals at specific times for special purposes. The Spirit fell upon prophets, kings, judges, even artists to empower their roles within the community. Now the Spirit was being poured out upon the entire community.

The Spirit became available to every woman and man who were making a decision to follow in the way of Jesus. The early community became known as "The Way." Often the Spirit came upon individuals at baptism, but at other times immediately at hearing the story of the life, death, resurrection and purpose of Jesus.

The connection to the lifeforce that human beings symbolically lost in the Garden of Eden was now being restored. Everyone who believed and gave themselves to this new way of being alive received the baptism, blessing, empowerment and energizing presence of the Spirit.

No longer were there one or two charismatic, empowered leaders. The Spirit empowered each member of the community to lead according to their particular gifts. Religion was no longer in the hands of and within the domain of the priest. The community became a priesthood of believers.

What people were receiving was not something new, it was something that had been lost as what we call civilization advanced. The Spirit, this web of connection existed before the creation of the Cosmos. Invisible fields of energy and power throb continually around us and through us. What humans have deemed as lesser forms of life are connected to and guided by forces beyond our present knowing. These "lesser" lives than ours; birds, mammals, fish, reptiles, insects, plants, are able to tap forces that guide them across great distances, endure harsh climates, sense minute changes, control heartbeat, sleep through seasons, awaken, feel, smell, hear, live connected to their environment beyond our comprehension.

The spiritual community that emerged from the life and teachings of Jesus lived within this new and ancient realm of connection. Members of the resurrected body of Jesus no longer feared death, not because they now believed in eternal life, but because they were participating in eternal life. They had through the Spirit become connected to the eternal web that transcended time. They were present with Christ prior to the beginning of the material universe and with Christ at the great coming together of all things that reached beyond the end of time. They lived moment by moment in the present because they were held in each moment by the Spirit.

Shortly before his death Jesus told his disciples that he would be more present with them, that they would more fully see him, following his death.

> "I will not leave you as orphans; I will come to you. After a little while the world will no longer see me, but you will see me; because I live, you shall also live." John 14: 18-19, NASB.

Jesus promises his followers that when he is gone a guide will be sent to them.

> "I will ask and the lifeforce will give you another helper, that will be with you forever; that is the Spirit of truth, whom the world cannot receive, because it does not know or see the Spirit, but you know the Spirit because the Spirit abides in you. From: John 14: 16-17.

The Spirit works with who we are and continually calls us to receive who we have been created to be. The Spirit reveals our strengths and weaknesses and helps us to accept the strengths and weaknesses of others. No one is better than us, no one is worse.

While there are many gifts associated with Spirit all pale in importance beside love. We are to seek spiritual gifts such as prophesy, teaching, gifts of healing, leadership, forms of assistance, discernment; but without love these gifts can easily become distracting and empty.

The fruit of the Spirit takes precedent over the gifts. If there is any measure of the Spirit's presence in our individual lives and our life within community it is found within the presence of the fruit of the Spirit; love, joy, peace, patience, kindness, generosity, faithfulness, gentleness, self-control.

The Spirits opens our eyes to others and to ourselves. We now see others and ourselves not only as they and we are, but as they and we were created to be.

Applying the Encounter to Our Lives

- Do you believe there is a dimension of connection and power that can guide, heal, inform, create, nurture, protect beyond what at this time can be seen or measured?

- Have you had an experience of connection to the Spirit? If so is there an example that you can share?

- How can one discern the spiritual gifts they have? Is there a spiritual gift that you have identified in yourself?

- What was the role of the Spirit in the early Christian movement?

- Consider the importance of the different aspects of the fruit of the Spirit?

- What was the role of the Spirit's presence with Jesus as he walked into the wilderness after the baptism?

- Why might the significance of the Spirit's presence diminish as the church grew more institutionalized?

Meditation Exercise

In the Early community of Jesus speaking in tongues became a common manifestation of the Spirit's presence. This was NOT a qualifying manifestation, not proof that the Spirit was present, certainly not a sign of spiritual maturity. Speaking in tongues was one way of going deeper into the mystery of connection to the lifeforce. The interpretation of tongues when speaking in tongues occurs during the gathering of the faith community is another aspect of the gift that we are not going to touch on here. Speaking in tongues is a form of prayer, a way of connecting to the Spirit significantly apart from the minds intervention. We open ourselves to the mystery of connection as we speak in a language of praise that is not an actual known human language.

> "Likewise, the Spirit helps us in our weakness; for we do not know how to pray as we ought, but that very Spirit intercedes with sighs too deep for words." Romans 8:26, NASB.

Set your timer to 14 minutes. Don't wait for the gift to come, speak the gift. Do not evaluate what is happening. Receive what is given, receive the moment.

The speaking is not apart from you, it is your voice, your decision to speak, your releasing what has always been there. You are in control of the gift.

It will not occur or go on without your intention. Receive the gift and the connection it brings.

If nothing happens experiment with this exercise another time. This is not a test of faith or measure of spirituality, it is an experiment within a larger seeking. This is not a primary gift. Joyfully receive it, joyfully walk away from it.

Repeat this exercise daily until the next encounter.

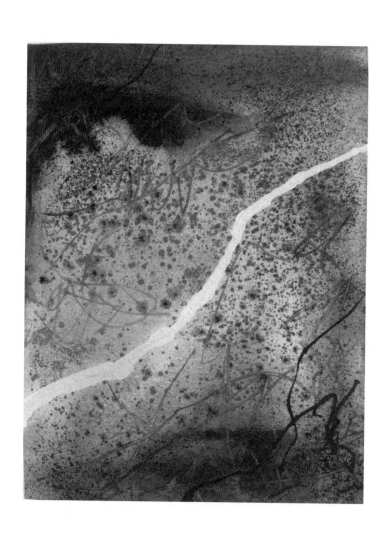

Hope

The path to hope and happiness is not what the world so often makes it out to be. As human beings we hope for many things; for health, happiness, prosperity, a long and happy life. If hope is based on how well things go for us in life then life becomes a gamble, much like playing poker. If we happen to draw the right cards and play them skillfully, things can turn out well for us. Conversely, if we draw the wrong hand about the best we can do is bluff and hope to get lucky.

Is it possible that hope is not grounded in what happens to us or doesn't happen to us so much as how we receive and work with what we are given? What is it in life that we can truly pin our hopes on? What is it within hope that we can with reason and faith truly expect to receive? What is the foundation of hope?

Hope can be fostered by a belief that there is a power, order and connection to the universe that unites every living thing. Hope then is grounded in belief that there is an order to the universe and that every created thing is connected to that order. What happens to us, no matter what it is, is caused by some effect of the creation's order. Human beings break from that order is the source of human suffering. The significance of that break is symbolically demonstrated within the first three chapters of Genesis. All humanity lives within the tragic consequences of our loss of union with the lifeforce that unites all creation. The foundational purpose of Jesus was to reunite us to the lifeforce and creation's order.

We live within a world of great and constant uncertainty. It can seem that everything around us is collapsing. Even the Earth's climate is deteriorating. Seemingly endless wars now affect our everyday lives. Something is very wrong that neither government nor religion is going to fix. Government and religion, as usual, have become a significant part of the problem. A communal sense that the Earth is teetering on the edge of apocalypse grows throughout the world.

Religious groups that provide the "right" answers, that believe they hold the only legitimate truth, that name the enemy and promise the only way to heaven, offer a delusional hope to cling to in this time of great uncertainty.

Political leaders who promise deliverance and clearly name the enemy offer a delusional hope to cling to in a time of great uncertainty.

There is one who supremely demonstrated the source and foundation of human hope. Jesus confronted the principalities and powers and exposed the illusion of the hope they offered. Jesus so threatened the powers of religion and the state that they united to put him to death on the cross.

The outcome of the ministry of Jesus appeared to have failed. He suffered a humiliating and torturous death. He had claimed that the lifeforce would not allow death to hold him. Jesus was resurrected from death. He came alive within those who believed in the life he offered, the life of self-sacrificing love, of picking up one's own cross, the power of stepping apart from the delusional promises of religion and the state. A new way of living became the foundational hope for a new kind of community.

Jesus did not sacrifice his life to get us into heaven after we die. This was not the foundational hope he offered. He opened us to the hope of a truly empowered way of living. The goal of the life of Jesus was both to expose false hope and to create a new reign, a new social, political and economic order based upon followers living with a whole new agenda for their lives. Eternal life was not a future hope, but a present reality.

> "I have said this to you, so that in me you may have peace. In the world you face persecution. But take courage, I have conquered the world!"
>
> After Jesus had spoken these words, he looked up to heaven and said, Father, the hour has come; glorify your son so that the son may glorify you, since you have given him authority over all people, to give eternal life to all whom you have given him. And this is eternal life, that they may know you, the only true God, and Jesus Christ whom you have sent." John 16:33-34, NASB.

Beyond Our Control—When Life Becomes Overwhelming

No matter how strong we may appear, how much faith we have, what our belief system is, there are things that can happen to us that overwhelm us. The list of possibilities is almost endless. Some of us inherit a predisposition for depression, anxiety, addiction and compulsive behaviors. No matter what our levels of endurance are, we all as human beings can encounter experiences beyond our ability to bear without great trauma.

Security is an illusion, created by human beings.

An almost continual experience of war through the past fourteen years is teaching us about the emotional toll affecting thousands of brave well-trained soldiers. Post-traumatic stress disorder (PTSD) has worked its way into our contemporary vocabulary.

Seemingly endless war has made us more aware of the price trauma can extract from our lives. PTSD has taught us that there are things that can happen to us that are beyond our natural strength and resistance to recover from.

Our lives can change in an instant. Catastrophe is part of the human experience. We all will die and along the way experience the loss of those we love; for all of us every kind of tragedy is possible.

Many of us are fortunate enough to escape major tragedies but many are not. Children die, accidents cripple for life, cancer is a word that induces fear, there is rape, murder, homelessness, and the list goes on and on.

Most people on Earth live in poverty, do not have enough to eat, have little access to health care, are subject to slavery and unimaginable abuse. Where is the hope under these conditions? There is no easy answer, but there is a solution that cannot be ignored. Jesus sought to establish a new form of social order and care based on love. Living every day with others who are seeking to live within an empowered love changes us and begins to change the world. This life of transforming love is our hope.

In The Midst of Suffering and Loss

We cannot avoid suffering and loss but we can live within a hope that transcends our suffering, a hope beyond healing. Jesus lived and died within that hope. Through his connection to the lifeforce that transcends decay and death, he embodied love. The by-product of love is hope.

> "Faith, hope and love abide, these three, but the greatest of these is love." 1 Corinthians 13:13, NASB.

Applying the Encounter to Our Lives

- Can you think of a time in your life when you were filled with hope? What were the circumstances?

- Can you think of a time in your life when you lost hope? What were the circumstances?

- What is your understanding of the basis for hope?

- What conditions in the world affect hope?

- What is the foundational reason for hope that Jesus offers?

- Did Jesus ever seem to lose hope?

- Can we as individuals, community members, nations and citizens of the world create a climate of hope?

- Can we experience a fullness of hope within our individual lives while others live in persecution and injustice?

- We live within a visible world of decay; nothing that we can see endures as it is. In what ways do human beings create false hope?

- Do you agree that an authentic connection to the lifeforce embodies love and that hope is a by-product of love?

Meditation Exercise

Set a timer for 15 minutes. Meditate upon Hope. Without thinking of reasons to be hopeful, attempt for the next fourteen minutes to reside within a spirit of Hope.

Breathe in Hope, exhale Hope. Let Hope fill your lungs at each breath. Let Hope expand your chest and move from your chest into your whole body. Let Hope fill your brain, flow into your arms and legs into your fingers and toes. Let your blood vessels flow with Hope. Let your six trillion cells fill with Hope. Let atoms, electrons and protons, charge your electrical system with Hope. Let the electrical charge around your body swarm with Hope.

As you exhale let Hope fill the room around you and flow from that room into your town, your city, your state, your nation, your world.

Repeat this exercise daily until the next encounter.

Heaven and Hell

Is there a heaven?

Is there a hell?

Is there an afterlife reward for those who live in the right way? Is there an afterlife punishment for those who live in the wrong way? These are questions that every human being comes to ask. These are questions that should be asked unless one decides to completely accept the answer given by their society, culture, nation or religion.

Throughout the history of humanity beliefs about an afterlife have been developed to answer apprehensions about death. What happens to me after I die? Will I see my mother and father again after they are gone from me? Will my husband, my wife, my children and I be reunited after death? Will my friends and family be reunited?

Is death the end of me?

Nothing is more common than our longing for wellness, for a life of health and comfort, of justice and peace. It is hopeful to believe that a place of comfort awaits us after death; especially as we face sorrow, injustice, suffering and decay in this life. Constructs of an afterlife can soothe our worry about our future. But there is a dark side within these constructs of heaven and hell.

The Dark Side

Throughout human history tribes, societies, nations and religions have used heaven and hell to control their members. Conformity to a cultures beliefs about heaven and hell gives great power to a relative few within that culture who hold power. Tribes of people who believe they are absolutely and uniquely right about their gods and their god's decrees, have been given license to perpetrate unspeakable horrors. Conquests and wars are empowered by the gods who hold the keys to heaven and hell. Those who conform are promised heaven; those who don't are assigned to hell.

A nation's soldiers are generally sent into battle with the blessing of religious functionaries whose job it is to assure heaven after a noble death. The 9/11 terrorists that flew two commercial airplanes into New York City's Twin Towers believed theirs was a mission ordained by God. They were promised immediate heaven after their noble death.

The crew of the Enola Gay, the World War II bomber that dropped the atomic bomb on Japan, unleashing hell in Hiroshima, were promised heaven through the blessing of a priest. The rightness of any cause is most often propped up by the promise of heaven and the fear of hell.

Does this mean that the way we picture heaven and hell are solely human constructs? Yes! The defined answer of what heaven is and what hell is, of who goes to heaven and who goes to hell, are invented by human beings.

Does this mean that there is no afterlife? No! We cannot know, despite the testimony of bestselling authors of lucrative books who have "temporarily" died and come back to tell us of their heavenly or hellish experience. Despite the claims of the sacred texts of the world's religions, we cannot know what awaits us.

Although we cannot know what will come after life, we can learn how to live the life we are given. Most religions give helpful advice in this regard. The danger is that religion continually seeks to manipulate its constituents by claiming a counterfeit certainty. In this light nationalism, secular humanism, atheism, capitalism, socialism, and communism are forms of religion.

This counterfeit certainty; this common human flaw of needing to believe that our tribe, our race, our nation, our religion, our political beliefs hold absolute truth and hold the keys to heaven and hell, rob us of the heaven that we can receive in this life, a heaven that begins now, that is eternal, that connects us to all that has been, to all that is, to all that will be. That heaven, that new realm is within us. This is what Jesus came to bring us into. When Jesus prayed; "May it be on Earth as it is in heaven," he was offering a way there in the present.

Entering Heaven

The New Testament is an amazing, miraculous compilation of writings based upon the message, life, death, resurrection, and ascension of Jesus. The New Testament offers an empowered way of living that is capable of transforming humanity; capable of saving humanity. The New Testament is lifeforce breathed.

While the New Testament offers the way, truth and life; the stumbling block for many is the realization that while the New Testament reveals truth, it is not necessarily literal and historic truth. In fact, it is most difficult to live within the Bible's deepest truth if one becomes lost in defending its literal truth.

For example; Genesis chapters 1, 2, and 3 do not explain a literal scientific truth. These chapters speak the truth of the human condition and predicament. To see these chapters as literal truth blocks entering their deepest meaning, their deepest truth.

The Gospel accounts are so contradictory that there is little illusion of literal truth. There are obvious additions created by the followers of Jesus throughout the decades after his death. These additions were drawn from the effects of Jesus on the emerging community life.

For example, there is no birth story in the Gospel of Mark, the earliest Gospel, and hardly a mention of the resurrection. There is no mention of Jesus' birth in John, the latest Gospel. The resurrection accounts are radically different in the four accounts of the Gospels. The writers are most concerned with transcribing transformational not literal truth.

The birth of Jesus was added to make Jesus a successor of King David, to make Jesus the Messiah. There was no world census. It is absurd to think that everyone returned to their hometown to be counted. King David's birthplace was Bethlehem. Joseph was connected to Bethlehem to reveal his lineage from David. At the same time Joseph is purported not to be the actual father of Jesus. Mary was purported to be a virgin who was impregnated by the Spirit of God. This was a common myth in its day, often used to claim the divinity of Roman emperors. Herein lies the message Matthew and Luke were trying to send. Jesus is a new kind of emperor, a new kind of king. Allegiance to this king transforms humanity. Believing in what is being said changes everything. Believing in the virgin birth makes the story magic; believing that the story radically intrudes on human history makes it transforming.

The birth story exposes the ultimate powerlessness of those who hold worldly power. The witnesses to this royal birth are poor shepherds on the low rungs of their society. The mystic wise men are not a part of the established religion Jesus is born into. Everything is being turned upside down.

Pregnant with new life Mary cries out:

> *"He has scattered those who were proud in the thoughts of their heart.*
> *He has brought down rulers from their thrones,*
> *And has exalted those who were humble.*
> *He has filled the hungry with good things;*
> *And sent away the rich empty-handed."*
>
> *Luke 1: 51b-53, NASB*

Believing that this story is historically accurate demands a level of naivety that can diminish its point. Living within the depth of this story's meaning opens us to the new reign of heaven now.

Heaven is a human construct, a symbol of what it would mean to be eternally held within the lifeforce. We cannot know what happens to us after we die. The idea of heaven can give us comfort; it is a way of believing that everything will be alright. It is a way of trusting life and the lifeforce that holds all creation together. Concern about going to heaven after we die can be a sign that we have not fully entered the new reign of heaven available to us in the present.

Hell

Hell, Satan, demons, evil spirits, are terms that human beings have developed to explain the presence and power of evil. To believe that these powers do not exist is to make oneself vulnerable to their destructive power.

Hell is a present reality with eternal consequences. Hell seeks to take up residence within our souls. The power of this place of enmity is that over time it can develop a stronghold within us. The full development of the stronghold of hell within our being can emerge and strengthen over years, over decades. Denial of the strongholds of hell can diminish our ability to perceive what is happening within us. Hell's strongholds can only be crumbled by seeing them and intentionally seeking their demise through prayer and fasting and opening ourselves to the new reign of heaven.

To believe that hell is a literal place where bad people end up after they die can open us to self-deception. Comfort can also be found through believing in a literal hell. Those who will not come to justice in this life will be punished in the next. There will be an accounting orchestrated by God.

The danger of believing in a literal hell is realized within our creation of a "them" and "us" mentality. Those not like us, those that don't believe as we do are going to hell, while those like us, who believe like us, are going to heaven.

Heaven

Heaven is a present reality with eternal consequences. Heaven seeks to take up residence within our souls. Heaven is a place of grace, peace and love that can over time strengthen its domain within us. The full development of heaven within our being emerges as we seek its dominion. Connecting to heaven's presence opens our spiritual eyes to the presence of justice and injustice, to the power of love and the pain of suffering. We seek a world in which it is on this Earth, as it is in heaven.

In our deepest being we learn to know heaven as a place of hope, a peace available to all yet not known, because not looked for. Heaven has been created by human imagination. It has been created and given a name because it is real; known in the depths of our being.

To believe that heaven is a literal place where good people go when they die trivializes its reality in the present, blinding our seeing.

To believe that the lifeforce of creation holds us eternally is life affirming, we trust eternity to the lifeforce.

A Final Reflection

We know so little. Ever increasing scientific knowledge reinforces how little we know of our vast universe. Scientists are now seeing evidence that there may be companion universes. It is possible that universes with entirely different properties intertwine with ours?

Fields of energy surround us whose functions we know little about. How might these fields relate to what we have called the Holy Spirit? How might intermingling universes coincide with what we have called heaven and hell? How might our understandings of the lifeforce that holds all of this together change and change us if we began to release our human centric interpretations of our place in the universe?

There is so much more to come if we don't destroy ourselves in the meantime. Heaven awaits but so does hell.

Applying the Encounter to our Lives

- Do you believe in heaven? Explain

- Do you believe in hell? Explain

- Do you trust the lifeforce to hold your present and future?

- Describe your picture of heaven?

- Describe your picture of hell?

- How are heaven and hell beyond physical places?

- How has religion at times abused understandings of heaven and hell?

- The following story has been used to foster belief in the literal existence of hell. Read and reflect upon this story.

  > Some men were digging a well in a village. They were not finding water at the level they had hoped. As they dug deeper and deeper they began to hear faint sounds beneath them. As they continued to dig the sounds intensified. They finally realized that they were hearing the screams of those in eternal hell beneath them wailing to be released. The men digging returned to the surface in a panic and quickly filled in the hole.

- How would you talk about heaven and hell to a questioning child?

- How do you think and feel about your own death? What gives you comfort? What is uncomfortable for you to think about?

- Do you live with a peace that everything will be all right?

- What is the new reign of heaven?

Meditation Exercise

Set your timer to 16 minutes. For the next 16 minutes enter heaven. Do not think about heaven, or what it would be like to be in heaven. Let your spirit enter a place of perfect peace, of justice for all, of hope and trust. Bathe your spirit in the perfect love of the lifeforce. All of the people you have ever related to are with you. Greet them in your spirit. Greet them in the spirit of the lifeforce, friends, family and enemies alike. Greet the poor and disenfranchised. Greet all beings. Greet the sun and moon, Earth, sky, and sea. Spend these minutes immersed in Heaven.

Repeat this exercise daily until the next encounter.

Story

The stories that we consciously and unconsciously adopt largely dictate our lives. There are multiple stories that we embrace through a lifetime. There are stories that we reject. There are stories that reveal and nurture deep truths. There are also stories that perpetuate and nurture great lies. If there is one true grand story, no one can receive it without shedding the stories we carry that defy it.

Our collective memories hold narratives that subtly and unsubtly support the superiority of the white race opposed to people of "color", the superiority of men over women, the superiority of our nation, of our religion. The conscious and unconscious list of such narratives holds degrees of power within each of us.

There is a nation's story, a white story, a black story; there is a story for the rich and a story for the poor, there are political stories, and religious stories, ethnic stories and generational stories.

New stories emerge within a lifetime. Old stories endure through decades, through and beyond centuries. Every generation forms its own stories. There are Depression stories, World War II stories, baby boomer, Vietnam, and Iraq stories, Generation X stories, Millennial stories, and more.

Each religion has its own story. Every branch of each religion has its own story. Every religion and every branch believes that its story is uniquely and exclusively true.

While religious stories can reveal deep truths, they have too often given support to the oppression of those who do not hold those same truths.

It is important to understand that what we recognize as true stories are true because of the power we give them. A story's historical and literal truth only holds power in our lives if we do much more than simply believe that they are historically true.

One can believe that George Washington, Abraham Lincoln, and Martin Luther King Jr. were great men who did great things. There is much that we know about them that is literally and historically true.

There is also a great deal of myth that is entangled within their stories. There is a mythology that has developed around these men that supports truths about who these men were beyond historical and literal truth. If we embrace the power of their mythological truth, something beyond just believing in their existence affects our relationship to them.

In the case of Washington, Lincoln, and King, each is a man. Few women have been raised to such prominence. Washington and Lincoln were white, the whiteness of their skin makes it easier for white-skinned people to mythologize them. The black skin of Martin Luther King makes it easier for black-skinned people to mythologize him.

Our stories are affected by who we are, where we were born and grew up, who our parents are, what decade we were born into, the religion, ethnic background, and race we were born into.

Mega Story

Is there a single grand story, a mega story, that holds the keys to the transformation of humanity into a new era of peace, love and justice for all? It is tempting for some of us with a Christian background to think that the Jesus story is the mega story for the salvation of the human race.

The trouble is, whose Jesus story, and which Jesus story are we talking about? Within a few years after his death numerous stories began to emerge. Over three hundred years later a group of powerful men gathered together to choose from the many stories that had evolved to form what would become the New Testament Cannon, the Christian Bible.

Would the stories chosen have been somewhat different if a group of women had come together? Were the stories and letters this group of men adopted or rejected chosen at least somewhat because of the institution they had created? There are many stories within the stories that were chosen. Each Gospel account focuses on a slightly different interpretation of Jesus. Is the true Jesus found in Matthew, Mark, Luke or John? Or is Jesus found only within the four Gospels seen as a whole?

Whose interpretation of Jesus will we choose; the Baptist Jesus or the Lutheran Jesus, the Presbyterian's Jesus or the Methodist's Jesus, the Anabaptist Jesus or the Episcopal Jesus, the liberal's story or the conservative's story, the progressive's story or the fundamentalist's story? Each group tends to believe that they alone hold the definitive truth. It is not surprising that so many are leaving Christianity in North America disillusioned and exasperated.

The problem with leaving is that more than an institution is vacated. In walking away, the story can also be left behind. A vacuum is created. That vacuum will over time be filled. New stories will consciously and unconsciously fill the empty space. At this particular time in history, the secular humanist story is becoming the foundational story.

The secular humanist narrative is too often an empty self-gratifying story, an amoral view of the world in which each person is a god unto themselves. Such a story demands a continual escape from its numbing emptiness. It should not be surprising that forms of addiction, whether technological or pharmaceutical, increasingly grip a world that has lost its story and in doing so has lost its purpose for living.

The Jesus story illuminates a way of living that seeks to transform and save the world from itself. To think that believing this stories literal truth will get one to heaven is to dangerously minimize its truth.

Jesus is about bringing heaven to Earth. The early followers of Jesus believed that the new reign of God would shortly be coming to Earth through a miraculous intervention of the Christ. The intervention of Christ was thwarted as "believers" turned their attention to a future Heaven.

The Ultimate Story

God creates Heaven and Earth, a physical world and a spiritual world. There is a break in the spiritual world when heavenly beings rebel against God. This insurrection fractures the goodness of God's creation. The effect on Earth is the shattering of human relationships and of human connection to God and creation.

To restore humanity, God comes into the world in the form of a baby, child, adolescent, adult and demonstrates a new way of being alive. God in Jesus has no wealth, no superpowers, no armies, no political clout. God in Jesus meets evil head on. Jesus both defies the powers that evil has constructed and submits to their illusion of control as he is tortured and executed on a cross.

The resurrection of Jesus exposes the ultimate powerlessness of greed, political and religious domination.

The followers of Jesus move from despair over what had appeared to be devastating loss, to a transformed, victorious way of living that Jesus had taught and modeled.

Through the ascension Jesus assumes his place in the eternal Heavens as past, present and future united through all of time and all of space.

At Pentecost a new age begins on Earth, as the Spirit of God is made available to all of humanity who will receive it. Now the living presence of Jesus walks the Earth through women and men who have been empowered to walk as He walked.

In submission to the Christ our mission in life is to live within the limitless healing power of divine love, non-violence, and mercy until it is on Earth as it is in Heaven.

Applying the Encounter to Our Lives

- Think about an incident in your childhood or youth that has continued to be a fond memory. Perhaps you have developed a story around this incident that you have frequently thought about or spoken of. Replay the story in your mind or write down a description of what happened.

  Now ask yourself; did this story occur exactly as you describe it? Would others involved remember it in the same way you do? Has this story, over time, taken on a meaning beyond what actually happened at that time? Is the story by itself as significant without your interpretation of how you were affected by it?

- Why is people's interpretation of the same story so often different?

- Do you carry a negative story? Is there a story that works against your wellbeing?

- What is the most significant aspect of the Jesus story for you?

- Why might the most significant aspect of Jesus' life be different for different people?

- How important is it for members of a community to agree on the interpretation of their most significant stories.

- What makes a story true?

- Is there an ultimate story for all humanity?

- How is your generational story different from that of your parents? From that of your children? How has your generational story affected your life?

- Is it important to pass down our significant stories to those who come after us?

- Is it important to be open to emerging stories?

Meditation Exercise

Set a timer to 17 minutes. Think of a significant story within your own life that continues to affect you. Perhaps you carry a story that makes you happy and feel content, or perhaps there is a story that continues to bring a feeling of loneliness and pain. Review the story in your mind. Allow your feelings around the story to emerge.

Start the timer. Stop thinking about the story. Allow the sense of the story, the emotions raised by the story to remain.

Bathe for the next seventeen minutes in the affects the story continues to have upon your spirit. Do not think about what happened or what is happening now. Do not evaluate. Let the sense of the story wash over you. Allow your spirit and soul to be ministered to.

Repeat this exercise daily until the next encounter.

Eucharist

Daily We Begin Anew

We awaken each morning to an opportunity for a new beginning. Within monastic and Orthodox Christian communities there is a daily Eucharist, a celebration of the communion they share with one another through their union with Christ.

The Eucharist, the partaking of the bread and wine, the Body and Blood of Christ, is a daily life renewing taking into oneself the living presence of Jesus, the embodiment of the lifeforce.

The disciples of Jesus had walked with him for three years. They had experienced his life changing teachings within each day. Throughout this time larger and larger crowds were pouring out of towns seeking to see and hear him. The Disciples and an ever-increasing number of women and men who followed him were continuously witnessing miraculous events and healings.

As the end of their time together on Earth drew near, the followers of Jesus could not fully see him. After three years of sharing meals together, experiencing his teachings and miracles, the disciples of Jesus did not really know him.

On the last day they would be together prior to his being taken by the religious authorities, condemned to death by the political authorities, tortured and executed, Jesus gathered his disciples for one last meal together.

Upon the occasion of this last supper together, Jesus prepared his disciples for all that would be coming. He promised that when he was no longer physically present with them he would be more fully revealed by the Spirit that would fill them.

Jesus then modeled the communion that would forever unite them to himself and one another. He began by washing their feet as a servant would wash the feet of dinner guests coming into a home. He washed the feet of Peter who Jesus warned would soon deny him, and he washed the feet of Judas who had already betrayed him.

Foot Washing (John 13:3-17)

Jesus had his disciples prepare a room for what he knew would be their last meal together on Earth. As Jesus entered the room his disciples were arguing among themselves over which one of them was the greatest. As they gathered for the meal Jesus assumed the role of the servant or at that time, of the slave.

Jesus laid aside his garments, girded himself with a towel, poured water into a basin and went about the room washing each of the disciples' feet, drying them with the towel wrapped around his waist.

Jesus has placed himself at the feet of those who had followed him as their teacher. He knows that Judas has betrayed him, that Peter will soon deny him, and that they will all soon abandon him in their fear; and still he kneels before each one and washes their feet.

He then explained to them how seeking greatness had no place in the community he was building, his body, that would remain on Earth. They were to be servants of one another and servants to even the least of those they would encounter.

Some Christian traditions practice a remembrance of this act of servant-hood prior to a communion service. They gird themselves with towels, a basin of water is circulated around the room as they wash one another's feet.

Bread and Cup

Jesus then took bread, broke it into pieces and gave it to his disciples as he told them that this was his body being broken for them.

Jesus poured wine into a cup and passed it among them as he explained that this was his blood being poured out for them. From now on though he could no longer physically be with them, he would be more fully present with them than ever before. In the eating of the bread and the drinking of the cup they would ingest his presence so deeply that his followers would from then on be his body on Earth. His presence would forever be experienced in the world through his life in them.

If received in a spirit of reverence and openness to their transformational power, these elements representing the Body and Blood of Jesus become supremely real in their power to transport us from death to life.

Our old selves, our Adam and Eve separated selves lived in an impoverished half-life, within an exhausting quest to fill a devouring black hole of emptiness, and unending hunger that could never be fully satisfied.

As we receive his Body and his Blood into ourselves, something deep within us is nurtured and satisfied.

Daily We Begin Anew

Lying down to sleep at night we surrender our actions, surrender our thinking, surrender our minds to sleep. Going to sleep can be seen as a ritual of death; the death of the day we have just lived through. In giving over each day as a kind of ending we have an opportunity to allow a new day to emerge fresh in the morning.

We awaken in the morning as from death to life. We awaken to a new day. Our arising each day can be seen as a resurrection. The old self is in the process of dying, the new self is in the process of becoming fully alive. Our body is continually transformed as we receive Christ anew.

It is not that we lose him and find him again in each new encounter. We open ourselves to a new depth of possibilities within each new day.

Although the Eucharist is a ritual of connection used daily within many Christian traditions, individuals and small groups can establish their own rituals. The point is to purposefully walk with intention, with openness to the lifeforce within each new day. When the day begins in this way one can be more conscious of the opportunities God continually brings before us.

A period of devotion upon arising that includes prayer, reading the Bible and devotional writings and memorizing Psalms, and scripture passages, can be a healthy beginning to each day.

Eucharist Service

The following is a celebration of communion designed for small groups engaging the materials in this book together.

Materials for Eucharist (Communion):

- Pita bread
- red wine
- a plate and small baskets for bread
- a chalice or bowl for wine
- a pitcher for wine
- table to hold elements

The seating might be arranged in a circle around the table or in a half circle toward the table. On the table arrange a pitcher holding the wine, an empty chalice or bowl to pour the wine into, a plate holding the pieta bread, a small basket to hold pieces of bread, and a small bell. As a chant or song is being sung or played two previously designated people from the group can go to the table and begin by tearing the bread into pieces and placing the pieces in a basket. Wine can then be poured from the pitcher into the chalice.

When the bread and cup are ready one of the designated persons can read or recite the following:

> When Jesus and the disciples had reclined at the table for their last meal together, Jesus took some bread and gave thanks. He then broke the bread and gave each disciple a piece, saying: This is my Body which is given for you, do this in remembrance of me.

A bell can be rung over the plate of pieces of bread saying:

> The Body of Christ broken for us.
>
> (Pause)
>
> Jesus took a cup of wine after they had eaten the bread and said to the disciples; This cup, poured out for you is the new covenant in my blood.

A bell can be rung over the chalice saying:

The Blood of Christ shed for us.

(Pause)

Whenever you eat this bread and drink the cup you proclaim the life Christ died for, you absorb into your being the life he lived to reveal.

The two people who have prepared the Eucharist can now be seated with the rest of the community.

One person at a time comes up and stands in front of the table. At this time the community recites in unison the person's first name and the following:

    __First Name__   , receive the Body and Blood of Christ given for you.

Following this invitation, the person standing before the table takes a piece of the broken bread and dips it in the wine. As she draws the bread to her mouth she can hold her free hand underneath the wine saturated bread. She can pause for a moment before the table in reflection and prayer as she eats the bread. Then she can go back to her seat. The next person may come forward when the previous person has gone back to their seat.

After each person who wishes has come forward the communion service can be closed in prayer:

May the Body and Blood of Christ release his presence within each of us and may our community serve as his body on Earth.

Close in song or chant.

Applying the Encounter to Our Lives

- If you have participated in communion services reflect upon your experience. How were you affected? If your experiences have varied in meaning consider why that might be.

- Should participation in communion be in some way limited? What might be criteria for participation?

- What are the implications of Jesus leading his disciples through the last supper before his Death and Resurrection? What was his purpose?

- Should Jesus have excluded Peter and Judas because of their denial and betrayal?

- To what degree do you believe the disciples understood what that last supper meant as it was happening? When might it have come together for them?

- Is ritual important in your life? Name ritual moments that come up through one's lifetime. What rituals have held special meaning for you?

- Think about your daily rituals. How might these daily, even very common rituals like brushing your teeth, bathing, exercise, preparing a meal, create a well-being both within and without?

- Do you practice daily spiritual rituals? Share with one another what has been meaningful in this regard. Note: We all fall short both in our spiritual practice and within daily life experiences. This should not discourage us. If you seek to adopt a new practice begin with something small that might increase over time.

- Do you believe in the power of prayer?

- Do you believe that a Eucharist service could be helpful to your group?

Meditation Exercise

Prepare a small glass of wine (an amount of a shingle swallow or two). Break a small piece of bread from a slice or a roll. Place both elements on a table. Sit comfortably at the table. Pick up the piece of bread. Hold it in the palm of your hand; the Body of Christ broken for you. Place the bread in your mouth, receiving his sacrifice, his grace, his love for you, his presence now within you always. Chew the bread slowly and completely. Swallow the bread, ingesting it into your body. Contemplate his presence within, as fully as possible allow him to fill you.

Pick up the small glass of wine. Hold it in your hand, the Blood of Christ shed for you. Take the glass to your mouth and drink. Hold the wine in your mouth for some moments before swallowing. If there is a small amount of wine remaining in the glass, finish it. The bread and the wine are now being absorbed throughout your entire body, touching every cell, every atom, into the depths of you. Receive.

Repeat this exercise daily until the next encounter.

Symptoms of Wellness

This guide does not constitute a program whose results can be easily quantified and measured. Spiritual healing and growth is a life-long process. Nonetheless, we have identified the following "symptoms" of wellness that can serve as guideposts on our journey.

- You have taken a fearless moral and spiritual inventory of your life. You have named demons that weigh you down, have power over you, and continually diminish your wellbeing. You have identified fears, behaviors and addictions that you continue to cling to. You have recognized and confessed to at least one other person the power these demons have over your life. You surrender yourself to the lifeforce that holds all of creation in its merciful care. In doing so you have recognized that your will to change your behavior is not sufficient and you are aligning yourself to a power beyond yourself.

- Through prayer, study, nurturing your relationship to people on a similar journey, fasting and meditation you seek the purging of all that holds you down. You open yourself to the presence, peace and power of Christ.

- Your gifts and passions are beginning to manifest themselves in ways that bless you and others. You have a clearer sense of the calling of the lifeforce to you personally. Everything that has ever happened to you, everything that you have ever experienced gives meaning to the present. You have a desire to use your gifts to help others. You trust the lifeforce to provide your ministry

- As you enter more deeply into the healing presence of Christ you more deeply commit yourself to easing the suffering and oppression of others in your community and throughout the world. You pay attention to the needs of people the lifeforce brings into your life. You give special attention to those regarded as the least in the world, the poor, the ill, the homeless, prisoners. You seek justice for the persecuted, the bullied, and the powerless.

- You see the sacred within everything the lifeforce has created. There is within you a Christ-like love for everything and everyone you encounter. You begin to identify the Creator's love in all creation.

- You are growing more acutely aware of the powers and principalities that seek to hold life in bondage. You experience the lure of the powers when you watch television, surf the Internet or cling to a cell phone. You understand the dominion of principalities when you go to a mall or walk into a school, give allegiance to a nation, political party or religion. You have been shifting your allegiance to the principal of non-violent inclusive love demonstrated by Jesus. You are learning to trust the way of Jesus, the new way of living that his life modeled and empowered.

- You are learning to live in quietness. You have broken with the exhausting pace of the world. You have found a place of silence that is refreshing to your soul. You have experienced sacredness in silence.

- You are living lighter; emptying your closets, drawers, and storage areas of things you no longer use or care about. You are becoming less dominated by technology. You are reducing your wants and examining what you have thought of as needs. A weight is being lifted from you.

- You are becoming childlike. You are beginning to realize the happiness of a child. You approach all relationships with a joyful childlike anticipation.

- You remember the acute pain and emptiness you once felt. The loneliness you so acutely felt is lessening. You no longer believe that you are alone in the world. You feel held by the lifeforce, by creation and by others that you are finding that are on their own journeys. You weep with those who weep. You laugh with those who laugh.

- A new health and quickness operates within your body, mind, and spirit. You feel a sense of vitality and health in the moment. You move with decisiveness. A new energy emerges in the depth of your being.

- You forgive yourself when you fall back into old habits, fears, self-centeredness, anxiety and depression. You have compassion for yourself and so are being taught to have great compassion for the failings of others. You now understand that the lifeforce will use you in your weakness and vulnerability. You honor your humanity. Your brokenness and your strength is a gift to your ministry. Wherever appropriate you have asked for forgiveness. You commit yourself daily to the new path you have taken.

- You carry in your person a love of family, a love of all people around you. You carry in your person a love for all creation. You can become almost overwhelmed by a sunset, the moon over the ocean, a bird's song in the morning, wind blowing through the trees. You live in a spirit of thankfulness for everything. You see the damaging effect of hatred, apathy, and injustice on all of creation.

- You have a sense that you are coming alive. Worship becomes a natural expression of your state of being. You sing and dance and praise. It is as if you have awakened. It is as if you have been born again.

Applying the Encounter to Our Lives

- Which symptoms of wellness do you especially identify with?

- Is there a symptom of wellness that you would add?

- Are there symptoms of wellness that you feel too easily elude you?

- Is there something in your life that triggers the erosion of your wellness?

- What aspect of wellness do you feel you most need to focus on?

- Have you identified a demon (a habit, addiction, mindset, fear) that too easily exerts control of your life?

- Are you forgiven? Have you received forgiveness? Have you forgiven?

- Is there a difference between guilt and shame?

- Do you believe that your relationship to others, especially those who are experiencing suffering and injustice, is critical to your own wellness?

Meditation Exercise

Set your timer to 19 minutes. Contemplate your wellness. If you have been in the midst of struggle lately, it may be difficult to feel well. Still, the foundation of wellness is more dependent on our state of mind than our state of affairs. So much as you find it possible open your body, mind and spirit in thankfulness to your wellness. This guide presumes that our ultimate wellness is dependent upon our trust, our faith that the lifeforce holds our past, present and future within the ultimate coming together of all things. All will be well.

Start your timer. Allow a spirit of wellness to wash over you for the next 19 minutes. Form your lips into a slight smile and hold that expression through this meditation; a gesture that signals your brain to relax, that things are well.

Repeat this exercise daily until the next encounter.

What Must Change

A personal letter to the faith community

Throughout my life, I have been blessed with a community of sisters and brothers who have cared about me. This community of seekers within and sometimes outside of the church has journeyed with me in seeking to live within the depths of Jesus Christ. I have been loved and within that love have been held accountable on a shared journey to be fully alive.

This journey of faith has continually led me to embracing new truths and new understandings that have often exposed old truths and old understandings that needed to be walked away from.

When Christianity was first being born the followers of Jesus had to step away from beliefs that were no longer consistent with the way, truth, life and love of Jesus. They had to step away from the religion that had begun to shackle them. They had to step away from scriptural understandings that had been followed for centuries. It must have been frightening to do so, and also exhilarating. In those early days of stepping apart from what they had previously assumed as "truth" it must have felt like shackles were falling from their wrists.

In every age the Spirit of God reveals new truth, sometimes making ancient understandings uncouth. The new reign of the lifeforce so often demands such changes.

It is difficult to believe that buying and selling human beings and holding them in bondage, as property, was at one time an acceptable, respectable practice in the United States. Of course black slaves were not regarded as fully human, not as "we" are, and the Bible was interpreted as clearly endorsing the practice of slavery.

When I was a child people of color were not allowed to stay in the same hotels as whites, they were not allowed to eat at certain restaurants, use white bathrooms or drink at certain fountains. My parents tried to teach me not to be prejudiced, but racial prejudice was so deeply ingrained within my culture that I at least unconsciously believed that "they" were different than "us". I didn't realize how subtly racism had been ingrained within me until as a young adult I became a member of The Church of the Brethren and encountered a group of people who were seeking to live within the way, truth, life and love of Jesus.

I was so deeply affected by this experience that after five years of teaching I enrolled in the Church of the Brethren seminary in order to give my life more fully to Jesus and to the community that sought to follow him.

After seminary I believed that I was being called to enter the ministry. At my very first interview with a Church of the Brethren congregation I was told by the search committee that their church did not accept blacks into membership. It was explained to me that things were slowly changing, that people of color were now part of the local fire department and probably the day would come when they would be welcome at church.

I was not dismayed, only deeply saddened. I remembered the racism that had almost imperceptibly resided within me.

When I look back now I am embarrassed by some views I once had related to women. I did not see how deeply sexism was ingrained within my culture and within me. Again it was through my encounter with Jesus and my faith community's encounter with me that my eyes began to be opened. My culture had blinded me to the constant degrading of women, the disrespect, and violence perpetrated on women. I now cringe at the many things that I once accepted as the way things are and the way God intended them to be. How could I have missed the radical acceptance and inclusion of women that Jesus so clearly and boldly expressed?

What in my life now do I accept too easily as the way things are and the way God intends them to be? What will I cringe at later in my life?

I now cringe at how I once believed that lesbian, gay, bisexual, and transgender people were "them" and not "us". My culture had taught me that "they" were unacceptable, to be despised and feared. This was ingrained within me from Jr. High on.

As so often is the case, my religion supported the cultural mandate and found the Biblical evidence that propped up the mandate. In doing so lesbian, gay, bisexual and transgender people were subjected to horrible, shameful treatment while religion generally cast a blind eye to their suffering, a closed ear to their cries. Again it was my community of sisters and brothers, who began to see the oppression, began to hear the cries, which helped me see and helped me hear.

No matter what aspect of sexuality any of us carry, all of us who seek to walk in the way, truth, life and love of Jesus need to submit our sexuality to his call to be fully and authentically alive within every aspect of our being.

Rejecting any person's sexual orientation is analogous to rejecting their skin color or their gender; both of which tragically continues to be done. Rejecting any person's sexual orientation is not a judgment we need to make. All of us, within any given sexual orientation need the guidance of the church as we seek to honor Christ in our behavior within our orientation.

On the journey to be fully alive will I one day cringe at the ease in which I now live while much of my world lives in desperate poverty? How will I now live in the midst of so much suffering, oppression and degradation?

Will I one day cringe at the poisoning of the very air we breathe and the water we drink, as I continue to live in the denial that my lifestyle largely contributes to this devastation?

The ever growing acceptance and glorification of violence, the entertainment value of violence in film and computer games, the titillation of murder and torture on television, the appeal of violence within sports, the willingness to do violence to our enemies; devalues human life and casts an ever darkening cloud over our future.

Smoking was at one time seen as an acceptable, enjoyable, even sophisticated practice. When I was a child certain brands of cigarettes were promoted over and against other brands by doctors on television ads.

We now know that smoking will lead to the deterioration of our bodies with likely horrible affects.

We are now beginning to see the devastating affects upon our bodies related to what and how we eat. Many of us are questioning how and what we eat related to our journey to be fully and authentically alive. We will in the near future look back upon much of the food we consume as we now look back upon smoking.

My hope for humanity and my hope for the Church that I love is that we could encounter the living Christ and the new era that he introduced; that we could look back on what has been while we look ahead at what could be and open ourselves to the new life Jesus continually calls us into.

The emerging awakening will change everything that we now think of as religion; from how we imagine God to how we read the Bible, experience community, and live in resistance to all that threatens justice, peace, and a life of sanity. The awakening will transform lives for the sake of human life on Earth. The life that Jesus taught, modeled and empowered will come to fruition within the awakened community.

Applying the Encounter to Our Lives

- Reflect upon how your opinions, beliefs and understandings have changed over the years. What changes seem most significant to your life at this time?

- At this point in your life what are you questioning? How might others be helpful to you as you seek more clarity?

- If you grew up in a home that observed the practices of a particular religion, how have your understandings related to that religion changed over the years? What has remained much the same?

- What needs to change for the sake of human life on Earth? What needs to change for the sake of all life on Earth?

- Is there an area of change that you feel led to actively support related to an immediacy of need?

- Was there a change that occurred in your life in which you felt released, freed, unshackled?

- How might shame and pressure from others be an obstruction to change?

- What in the Encounter 20 letter do you feel most connected to? Least connected to?

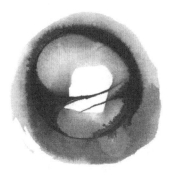

Meditation Exercise

Set your timer to 20 minutes.

In the 21st chapter of the New Testament Book of Revelation, a new Heaven and a new Earth are envisioned. The first Heaven and the first Earth have passed away. Every tear will be wiped away, there will no longer be death, no longer mourning, or crying, or pain. All that we have previously known is being made new.

Within the next 20 minutes, give yourself to the vision of a new Earth. What might it mean to your spirit to open yourself as completely as possible to a new Earth? Try not to picture and think about all the changes. Allow your spirit to reside in the newness.

Repeat this exercise daily until the next encounter.